BBC Children's Books
Published by the Penguin Group
Penguin Books Ltd, 80 Strand, London, WC2R 0RL, England
Penguin Group (Australia) Ltd, 250 Camberwell Road, Camberwell, Victoria
3124, Australia (a division of Pearson Australia Group Pty Ltd)
Canada, India, New Zealand, South Africa.

Published by BBC Children's Books, 2011
Text and design © Children's Character Books, 2011

001 – 10 9 8 7 6 5 4 3 2 1

Written by Dan Newman and Sam Philip
Designed by Dan Newman, Perfect Bound Ltd

ISBN: 978-1-40590-795-8

Printed in China

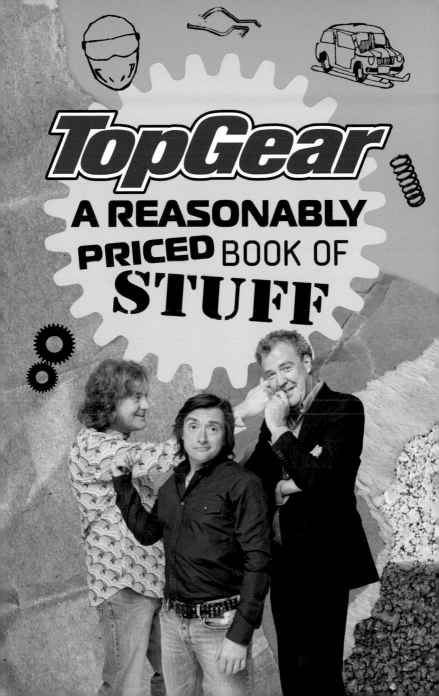

TopGear

A REASONABLY PRICED BOOK OF STUFF

Contents

Introduction

If you've been watching *Top Gear* for a while, you may have got the impression it's a show about three middle-aged men mucking about. That's kind of true, but there's a lot more to it than that. Quite often, for instance, you find out some facts about cars. Or foreign countries. Or celebrities. Or rockets, caravans, camping, satnavs, boats, tunnels, motorbikes, hats, insults, limited-slip differentials, explosions, food and road signs. If you're the kind of person that likes to know things, this is all *very* exciting.

So a reasonably-priced book jam-packed full of all those kinds of facts seemed like a very good idea. Here it is. **Enjoy**.

But... there's a problem. It turns out that, in real life, almost all this information is useless. No one else really *cares* about the power-to-weight ratio of the Bugatti Veyron. You'll never get a test at school on the M25. When you grow up, you won't get promoted for knowing where Koenigseggs come from. Sorry.

Actually, that's what *Top Gear* is **really** all about. Being interesting, but **useless**. Being ambitious, but **rubbish**. Which means *Top Gear* is just like the entire history of motoring – full of ideas that seemed great at the time, but turned out to be utterly stupid. That's the price you pay for trying: sometimes, you get it wrong. You want to develop the Bugatti Veyron, but you end up with the Morris Marina. Never mind. Laugh about it, and try again. Just like Jeremy, Richard and James.

Some useless things

A chocolate teapot
A glass trampoline
A rubber hammer
A paper canoe
A snooze button on a smoke alarm
A cat flap on a space rocket
Jeremy's sense of restraint
Richard's sense of taste
James's sense of direction
The Stig's mobile phone

The Collected Thoughts of Jeremy Clarkson

[After riding a motorbike across Vietnam] I've always said that if my children buy a bike, I'll **burn** it. If they replace it with another one, I'll burn **that one** too. Now when they buy a bike, I will completely understand. And *then* I'll **burn** it.

Why don't **all** cars have no doors? When I come to power, I'm going to make it a rule, because this is just **better**.

[The best car of 2005] It's not a democracy, it's a **dictatorship** – and I'm dictating that the Aston Martin V8 Vantage is the winner.

Caravans. **Get out of the way!** Pull over once in a while, once every 300 miles! Pull over! **Please!** Get out of the way! Pleeaase! Stay in a hotel next time! **Pleeeeeaaaase!**

I'm sorry, but when we come to power, caravanning is going to be banned, and that's it.

Absolutely no idea.
No, genuinely, I have **no idea** how an engine works. People have sat me down and said, petrol goes in, then pistons go up and down, and somehow you go along. **How does that happen?**

If I have a car in front of me – Richard, you'll identify with this – I **need** to be past it. It's the **most** important thing. **You** are in front of me, I want to be where **you** are.

[Putting the Smart car on the Cool Wall] You're wrong, I'm always right; it's going **there** because I know **everything**.

[About the Nissan Juke] You buy a car because you want something that's fast, or something that's cheap, or something fast. How many people do you know that say 'I want to buy a car that's absolutely stupid'?

You know Infiniti? No, not endless time and space, the Japanese car maker. They're Datsuns with a bit of velvet in them, basically.

Heathrow, if you're watching this, you're **pathetic**. Anybody in a meeting who says 'The reason it was shut is…', *sack him*. There is **no reason** why it was shut, because it *isn't* difficult to clear a runway, it just **isn't**.

[The BMW M3] It's available with a matt finish, which is as **cool** as buying some skinny jeans, and then making an **app** about them.

The government says that because it only has *three* wheels, it's not a car, and as a result you save £55 a year on your tax disc. Now obviously, the **best way** of exploiting this loophole is to take a wheel **off** your car and drive around on the other three. But we **don't** recommend that.

With my new anti-capsize solution in place, I knew **nothing** could go wrong. And I knew that *right up to the moment* when it **did**.

11

The Inventive Outbursts of Richard Hammond

[About the Marina] I **guarantee** that nothing exciting, vibrant, dynamic, new, creative, hopeful or beneficial in any way to humanity has **ever** been done, thought of or driven to in that drab, dreary, entirely beige wilfully awful pile of **misery**.

How could you **not** like the GT2? You great fat, balding, useless, hopeless, bandy-legged, bubble-haired, pointless, talentless, gutless, cowardly, witless lump of suede-shoe wearing, daft jean-wearing **idiocy**.

Lamborghini is owned by Audi. So the Germans do the actual building of the cars, and then they let the Italians do the brochure...'It's got a **MILLION** horsepower! Does 100,000mph! Is **invisible!** And it's got **cannons!**'

This [Volvo V70 estate] is a box for carrying your airbags around in. It's driven by men in beige trousers who have a problem **stopping** when they finish weeing.

All Lexuses are beautifully made and impeccably engineered to achieve unparalleled levels of **dullness**.

Have you ever noticed, watching Jeremy do anything practical, it's like watching an orang-utan? He's happy, but **confused**.

[To James] Now you've confused **yourself**, you poor old goat!

[On caravanners] Every summer they arrive, **ruining** our roads, just so they can pull up side by side with their new best friends. And pee in a bucket.

[To himself] '**Remember** to brake at sixty. **Remember** to brake at sixty, you **stupid** boy.

[In a tent in Bolivia] What's that? Aaagh! Ah! Stick insects! Something's honestly landed on my head – oh, **what is that?!** There's something that just flew in my hair and it's squeaking at me and it's **big**!

What's the point of insuring an American's head? There's **nothing** in it!

[About the VW Beetle] That is a **wretched**, awful miserable, spluttering, puttering, slow, noisy, ugly piece of hateful **misery** and the worst attempt at a people's car the world has ever suffered.

Have you met Jeremy Clarkson? Big tall feller. Curly hair. Idiot.

13

The Rather Impressive Knowledge of James May

It requires something we don't normally feature on *Top Gear*, which is very accurate calculations. **Everything** – the weight of the car, the speed of the car, the angle of the ramp – it all comes together in a gigantic ball of **arithmetic**.

I think this modern obsession with horsepower is absolutely **idiotic**. You see, a simple, light, well-sorted **classic** will be more than a match for some youth car with 5,000 horsepower and a big stereo.

Good News! No, wait – it's better than you think. The new Dacia... **DUSTER** *is* coming to the UK!

This is it – the Moon Buggy Mark 2. A car for outer space. This is **much** more exciting than something like a Veyron SS or a Ferrari 458. Those are just *Earth cars*.

The only thing I keep in my car is a little brush for cleaning dust out of the switches. And I always like to keep the air vents lined up so they're symmetrical.

There's something **tragic** about bottom-of-the-range. You sit there in a world of velour looking at a little plastic-covered slot on the dashboard where you **know** there would be a switch if this was the posh version. And you think, if I'd just paid a **bit** more attention at school, if I'd just worked a **bit** harder... I'd have air conditioning.

Age, **experience**, tweed and a little bit of facial hair is what it takes to win at hill-climbing.

Aber ja, natürlich Hans nass ist, er steht unter einem Wasserfall.*

The issue is the **air**, which has genuine substance when you're trying to drive through it. The faster you go, the thicker the air effectively becomes. At 10mph, it's like aerosol whipped cream. But at 200mph, it's more like a very thick treacle. And at 250mph, it's like trying to drive through a very thick **fruitcake**.

Cars that drive themselves were invented ages ago. They're called **taxis**.

I've got a handbook for an early 1970s Datsun, and right in the middle of the instructions for adjusting the seat it says '**Cement the driver's arm to the handle.**' And in the index, under H, is '**How to open the bonnet.**'

Here's a proper piece of British ingenuity: a bloke called Geoff, he's made a steam-powered bicycle after thirty years' work. He started work on it in 1972. Roughly **250 years** after the steam engine was invented.

Right. I've been looking in the *Guinness Book of Records*. It doesn't actually say that I have to use a car to tow the caravan. So instead I've decided to rely on the most powerful engine in the universe. **Gravity.**

It's fine. I worked it out, according to Archimedes. When a body is partially or wholly submersed in water it experiences an **upthrust** equal to the weight of the water **displaced**.

That. Won't. Work.

---

* The only German James knows: 'Naturally Hans is wet, he is standing under a waterfall.'

Five of the World's Most Dangerous Roads

The boys survived one of the deadliest roads on Earth in Bolivia, but they'd be well advised to steer clear of this lot...

The Lena Highway, Russia

This 600-mile highway, running from Moscow to the icy northern city of Yakutsk, is built from mud and frozen solid for ten months of the year. During July and August, though, it becomes a giant bog, trapping cars for days. It's also popular with kidnappers!

The Trollstigen, Norway

No, it's not named after *Top Gear*'s white-suited racing driver, but this Norwegian mountain road is just as mysterious and scary. Its name means the Troll-Ladder, and it consists of a dozen hairpin bends haring up a sheer mountain face, with terrifying drops off the edge!

Espinazo del Diablo, Mexico

In Spanish, that means 'The Devil's Backbone'. A mountain pass connecting the cities of Durango and Mazatlan in central Mexico, this narrow road is filled with huge lorries, charging out of control down its steep slopes. With 1000-foot drops to the valleys below, that's a recipe for brown trousers!

Richard in the Porsche

Jeremy in the Lambo

James in the Aston

The Stelvio Pass

This amazing set of hairpins was discovered by Jeremy, James and Richard when they set off in search of Europe's greatest driving road in the Aston Martin V8 Vantage N24, Lamborghini Gallardo Superleggera and Porsche 911 GT3. It might be fun to drive, but watch out for the edge!

Guoliang tunnel road, China

Just thirteen local villagers carved this scenic-but-deadly tunnel into the mountainside in the 1970s. The views across the mountains are spectacular, but you don't want to meet a truck coming the other way!

Musical Instruments *Top Gear* has Destroyed

The Top Gear boys love music. Unfortunately, they seem to hold a bit of a grudge against the instruments that produce it...

James's grand piano

One of the legs from Captain Slow's beloved piano fell off before the boys' lorry hill start challenge. Thankfully, James crashed into it, so he never found out!

Jeremy's drum kit

Jeremy successfully managed a hill start in his lorry, avoiding his precious set of drums. So James and Richard destroyed them anyway...

Jeremy's other drum kit

Jeremy managed not to destroy his drum kit in the accelerate-to-60mph-and-brake-within-200-metres challenge. So Richard ran over it, just to be on the safe side...

James's other piano

Could James's rear-wheel drive Ford Capri accelerate to 60mph and then slow to a stop within 200 metres? Er, no. Here's what happened to the piano he bought to replace the first one...

Several other pianos

After upsetting the Morris Marina owners club by setting fire to one of the classic British Leyland cars, the boys bought a pristine Marina to preserve for eternity. Unfortunately, a grand piano somehow fell on it on the *Top Gear* track. Then it happened again, in France. And again! What *is* it with Marinas and pianos?

What WILL Richard Eat?

Richard is a faddy Brummie. There's a lot of things he doesn't eat. The only things we've actually seen him eat include:

Cornish pasties and sausage rolls
Sliced white bread
Crisps
Rice Krispies (with chopsticks, in Vietnam)
Cornflakes
Maltesers
Custard creams
Jaffa cakes
Chocolate biscuits
Swiss roll
Battenberg cake
'Value' sausages
Scotch eggs
Crème eggs
Pork pie
Yogurt

I think this is some sort of squid thing, with weird paste.

OK, well you can have crab with–

Razor clams in–

Don't like squid.

Don't like crab.

Don't like clams.

How to Drive Across the Desert

On their big trip across the Middle East, the boys decided it'd be an excellent idea to sneak through the Syrian desert to avoid attention. But they soon discovered that driving in the desert is more difficult than it looks. Here's what you need to know to make sure you don't get stuck in the sand.

Use a 4X4

This was the boys' first mistake. A car with proper four-wheel drive and good ground clearance will cope much better with boggy sand than, say, a tiny rear-wheel drive roadster. Even if it's got six wheels and an egg-frying device on the back.

Distribute your luggage evenly

If you've got too much weight on one corner of the car, that wheel will push down into the sand and you'll get stuck. So make sure you spread your luggage – and passengers – around the car. If, for example, you've got an enormous, shouty, curly-haired man on board, put plenty of ballast on the other side to keep things balanced!

Deflate your tyres (a bit)

Releasing some air from your tyres will give them a wider area of contact with the sand, spreading your car's weight out and giving more grip. But make sure you don't let them down too far, or you'll be even more stuck than you were before!

Drive at a steady speed

In the desert, maintaining your momentum is key. If you slow down too much, you'll sink in the sand and won't be able

to get started again. But get too fast and you won't be able to avoid ruts and bumps... or camels!

Make gentle turns

If you try to take a corner too quickly, your car will dive into the sand and you'll have to dig your way out. Make wide, sweeping turns... and stay calm!

Go straight up and down dunes

You should never drive 'across' a steep slope, with one side of the car higher than the other. Only go straight up or down dunes, keeping the left- and right-hand sides of the car level. This should prevent you from tipping over and ending up on your roof!

Stuck? Don't panic

If you get bogged down in the sand, the worst thing you can do is to keep pushing the accelerator – the wheels simply dig further and further down! First of all, try to gently reverse out along your own tyre-tracks. If the car still won't budge, let down your tyres even further and get your mates to give you a push. If that doesn't do the trick, well, you'd better hope someone is nearby to tow you out of your hole!

Pack lots of water

Deserts are very dry. And very hot. And very empty. If you get truly wedged in the sand, it'll be a long time before anyone arrives to dig you out. Make sure you take plenty of supplies with you – and charge up your mobile phone before you go!

And, most importantly...

Don't attempt to cross the desert with a pair of buffoons!

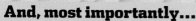

Questions No One Had Asked Until *Top Gear* Provided The Answer

How many motorbikes can a double-decker bus jump over? Three. It then crushed eleven others.

Can grannies do doughnuts? Yes, eventually.

Can you make a Bond car full of gadgets for £300? Kind of... a bit... no.

Can grannies do handbrake turns in a Mini? Ooh yes.

What do you have to do to a Lada Riva to make it nice to drive and cool to be seen in? Give it to Lotus for 1000 hours, and spend £100,000 replacing almost everything.

Can Ford's World Rally Championship pit team rebuild a rally car faster than four women can get ready for a night out? They can, a lot faster.

Can you tow a caravan at 120mph? Yes, but it will break your car. To get a caravan moving *really* fast, drop it from a crane.

Can a Volvo 240 jump over five caravans? No. Two, yes – but not five.

Can you wear a wig in a convertible? Yes, if it's a cheap one. Or if the car has wind deflectors.

How much faster will a Jaguar XJS go if you strip off all the panels to save weight? Not much – a second or so.

Will it go faster if you add a nitrous injection system? Ooh, yes. Loads.

Can a nun drive a monster truck? Yup.

Can you play darts with cars? Yes, if you put a caravan on the bullseye.

Is it safe to get struck by lightning in a car? Yes.

Can you power a car with LPG made from poo? Yes, but it costs too much to be worth it and it smells.

Is the jetwash from a Jumbo Jet really that powerful? You bet it is.

Can you parachute into a moving car? Amazingly, yes – but it is VERY difficult.

How many bouncy castles can an ice cream van jump over? None, of course. Don't be stupid.

Can you play conkers with caravans? Yes, if you paint them brown.

Can you get round the Nürburgring in under ten minutes… in a diesel car? Yes, just, if you are Jeremy; yes, easily, if you are Sabine Schmitz.

Can a stretch limo jump over a wedding party? Partially yes, mainly no.

Can Jeremy drive fast enough to avoid Army snipers? No.

Can a Mini jump further than a skier? No, but it had a damn good try.

Can you make real cars into radio-controlled ones? Yes, but get a girl to drive them (rather than James or Richard).

Can the Stig set the non-existent indoor speed record? Yes, he can.

Does a G-Wiz make a decent radio-controlled car? No. Of course not.

What was the first car ever made to have the controls in the places we think are normal? Cadillac Type 53 from 1916, and copied by the Austin Seven.

Can *Top Gear* break the non-existent world record for the backwards car jump? Kind of.

Can *Top Gear* beat *Fifth Gear*'s distance for jumping a car while towing a caravan? No.

Can Jeremy beat the Army at British Bulldog? Not once they get their guns out.

Can Jeremy drive eight miles in a Reliant Robin without crashing? No.

Fastest Stars in a Reasonably Priced Car

It's hardly fair to compare the much newer, nippier Kia Cee-apostrophe-d to the thrashed Chevrolet Lacetti and the frankly prehistoric Suzuki Liana. But let's do it anyway. Here's some top threes, and the (hold thumb and forefinger to forehead) LOSER in several categories.

Name	Car	Time	Comment
American actors			
Tom Cruise	Cee'd	1.44.2	Ended on two wheels
Andy Garcia	Cee'd	1.46.1	With impressive facial hair
Jeff Goldblum	Cee'd	1.49.0	In 3rd gear the whole time
David Soul	*Liana*	*1.54.0*	Broke two gearboxes, coasted last bit
Actresses			
Cameron Diaz	Cee'd	1.45.2	
Jennifer Saunders	Lacetti	1.46.1	
Billie Piper	Lacetti	1.48.3	
Kristin Scott-Thomas	*Lacetti*	*1.54.0*	
British actors			
Nick Frost	Cee'd	1.44.5	
Simon Pegg	Cee'd	1.44.9	
Rupert Grint	Cee'd	1.45.5	
Brian Cox	*Lacetti*	*2.01.0*	
Musicians			
Jay Kay	Lacetti	1.45.81	Did a little dance of joy
Brian Johnson	Lacetti	1.45.9	
Justin Hawkins	Liana	1.48.0	
Geri Halliwell	*Liana*	*1.55.4*	Wet
Presenters			
Kevin McCloud	Lacetti	1.45.87	
Peter Jones	Cee'd	1.45.9	
Simon Cowell	Lacetti	1.45.9	
Richard Whiteley	*Liana*	*2.06.0*	

Sportspeople

Boris Becker	Cee'd	1.45.9	Wet
Usain Bolt	Lacetti	1.46.5	The fastest on two legs
Dame Ellen MacArthur	Liana	1.46.7	Get her in the Cee'd!
Amy Williams	*Cee'd*	*1.50.9*	Wet

Comedians

John Bishop	Cee'd	1.42.8	Amazing!
Jimmy Carr	Liana	1.46.9	
Rory Bremner	Liana	1.47.9	
Jimmy Carr	*Lacetti*	*2.08.9*	Spun off the track

Models

Jodie Kidd	Liana	1.47.7	
Peta Todd	Cee'd	1.49.9	Wet
Jordan	*Liana*	*1.52.0*	

F1 drivers

Rubens Barichello	Liana	1.44.3	
Nigel Mansell	Liana	1.44.6	
Lewis Hamilton	Liana	1.44.7	Wet and oily
Mark Webber	*Liana*	*1.47.1*	Very wet

Irishman

Patrick Kielty	Lacetti	1.48.0

Welshman

Michael Sheen	Lacetti	1.46.3

Scot

Ewan McGregor	Lacetti	1.48.0

Australian

Eric Bana	Lacetti	1.47.5	Wet

Gallifreyan

David Tennant	Lacetti	1.48.8

Average time   1.50.5

Most common time   1.54.0   Driven by Martin Kemp, Stephen Fry, Kristin Scott Thomas, David Soul, Alan Davies, Rich Hall, Ross Kemp, Tara Palmer-Tomkinson...

The *Top Gear* Track

Top Gear *is filmed at Dunsfold Aerodrome, near Guildford in Surrey, in a big old draughty aircraft hangar. There's lots of room to park cars, and no awkward steps. And right outside are... two runways.*

The clever chaps at Lotus painted lines and stacked tyres to mark out a racetrack on these runways. It's short (only 2.82km /1.75miles) and twisty, in a kind of long, squashed figure-of-eight. It doesn't really matter what a car's top speed is, or how fast it gets to 60mph – there's too many corners on the TG track to really get going. It's a real test of every aspect of a car, from tyres to brakes to weight to balance.

The slowest star (Richard Whiteley) averaged 50mph round the course. But the fastest stars, Rubens Barichello and John Bishop, only averaged 60mph! The Ariel Atom V8 only had to average 84mph to get to the top of the Power Laps board.

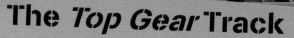

Willson Ben

Follow-through

Hammerhead

So what's the route?

You start on a narrow service road near the edge of the airfield. As you pull away with squealing tyres, there's a little bend to the right, then to the left – just to get you started. Then a hard corner to the left onto the end of one runway – **Willson Bend**. Just as you start to

really get going, you have to swing over to the left before squealing past the tyre wall to the right – **Chicago**. Floor it and head towards the end of the second runway, where the tricky **Hammerhead** is marked out.

Sharp left, then a long right – if your car tends to understeer or oversteer, it'll show here. Then as fast as you can (on the longest straight section) towards the **Follow-through**, a terrifying right-hander that will send the car screaming onto the runway again. (Here's where you may need new pants – hence the name.) Past the tyre wall again at top speed, making the remote camera wobble, but this time round to the left on **Bentley Corner**. The **Second-to-last Corner** is a left onto the service road, a wide turn which gets tighter. Most of the stars are going way too fast as they approach this, which is good for laughs. The last corner is a right-angle (to the left) – swing the wheel hard over and hang on, as your tyres may well leave the tarmac. It's named **Gambon**, after the actor that first turned the Reasonably-Priced Car into a two-wheeler here. A final, desperate lunge ... and **across the line!**

> *Why don't they hold races on the TG Track?*
> **Because it's a figure-of-eight – cars would crash!**

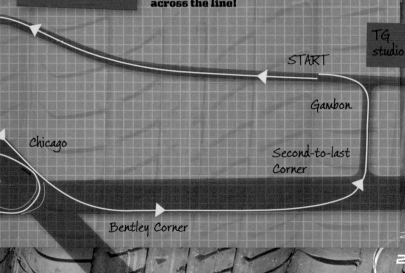

TG studio

START

Gambon

Chicago

Second-to-last Corner

Bentley Corner

Ten Cheap Cars That Aren't Rubbish

In 2009, the boys set out to discover some new cheap cars that weren't rubbish. They found the Proton Satria Neo, Chevrolet Aveo and Perodua Myvi, all of which are definitely rubbish. But this lot are actually pretty good...

Fiat 500

Cost: £9,500

Why it's not rubbish: Looks like it's come straight from the 1960s. The 1960s were cool.

Alfa MiTo

Cost: £12,000

Why it's not rubbish: Because it's an Alfa, and petrolheads aren't allowed to hate Alfas.

Skoda Roomster

Cost: £11,000

Why it's not rubbish: The fastest car round the *Top Gear* test track... with a Great Dane in the back!

Honda Jazz

Cost: £11,000

Why it's not rubbish: Brilliant Japanese engineering – with room for your granny on the back seat.

Fiat Panda

Cost: £7,800

Why it's not rubbish: Because James May owns one. Hang on, that's not a good thing, is it?

Hyundai i10
Cost: £7,700
Why it's not rubbish: Because it makes you drive like you're in a James Bond car chase...

Ford Fiesta
Cost: £10,000
Why it's not rubbish: It can outrun Corvette-driving baddies through a shopping centre and survive a Royal Marine beach landing!

Renault Twingo
Cost: £7,700
Why it's not rubbish: You can fit a whole Ross Kemp in the boot.

Citroen C1
Cost: £8,500
Why it's not rubbish: Survived nearly as long as Hammond in a deep freeze chamber, and warmed up quicker afterwards.

VW Fox
Cost: £7,500
Why it's not rubbish: Tiny Volkswagen turns out to be very good at car football...

Stigs Around the World

The Top Gear *boys have encountered many Stigs on their travels around the world. Meet the family...*

Black Stig

Only survived until the end of the first series, when he drove off the end of an aircraft carrier, never to be seen again.

Fat Stig

Discovered on the boys' American road trip, Stig's American cousin set a trio of lap times in their second-hand cars.

African Stig

Found in Botswana. Wore nothing but driving shoes, gloves, helmet and a loincloth. Refused to set a lap time in Jeremy's Lancia Beta after the rusty Italian car wouldn't start.

Rig Stig

Proved it **is** possible to power-slide a 5,000-pound truck during the boys' Big Lorry Challenge. Like all seasoned truckers, had a very tanned right arm.

White Stig

The legend of the *Top Gear* test track. Some say he is illegal in seventeen US states, and he blinks horizontally...

Vegetarian Stig

Tested *Top Gear*'s homemade electric car, the Hammerhead Eagle iThrust, 2009. Died shortly after.

German Stig

Tested *Top Gear*'s 'ultimate track day cars' around the EuroSpeedway in 2010. Identical to White Stig in every way apart from one: a mullet.

How to Make a Manly Smoothie

Want to know how to make a smoothie that'll put hair on your eyeballs? First, you'll need the V8 blender from page 136. Then follow this recipe.

Ingredients

Beef: Six or seven large chunks, each the size of a man's fist, should do the job. No problem if it still has bones in it.

Chillis: A few handfuls. Don't worry about removing the seeds.

A brick: For added crunch.

Tabasco sauce: A glassful.

Worcestershire sauce: Another glassful.

Bovril: Enough to fill the largest container you have in the house. Even if it's a bath.

Method

1. Stuff all the ingredients into the blender.
2. Lock the lid down as tightly as possible.
3. Strap on a pair of pink fluffy earmuffs to protect against the fearsome noise of the V8.
4. Fire up the blender and stand well back!

Warning: This recipe is messy, dangerous and probably poisonous. Please don't try it at home. Or, in fact, anywhere.

AWFUL!

I'm **not** sure this works!

Some Say...

He lives in a tree...
He roams around the woods at night foraging for wolves...
He never blinks...
He blinks horizontally...*
He sleeps upside down like a bat...
He sleeps inside out...
He naturally faces magnetic north...
His sweat can be used to clean precious metals...
His ears aren't exactly where you'd expect them to be...
His ears have a paisley lining...
He has a digital face...
To unlock him you have to run your finger down his face...
He has a full-size tattoo of his face – on his face...
His voice can only be heard by cats...
His tears are adhesive...
He has webbed buttocks...
All his legs are hydraulic...
He has two sets of knees...
His skin has the texture of a dolphin's...
His heart ticks like a watch...
His heart is in upside down...
His teeth glow in the dark...
His earwax tastes like Turkish Delight...
His breath smells of magnesium...
The outline of his left nipple is exactly the same shape as the
    Nurburgring...
On really warm days he sheds his skin like a snake...
In the autumn, all his arms go brown and fall off...
If you lick his chest it tastes exactly the same as piccalilli...
His crash helmet is modelled on Britney Spears' head...
He's confused by stairs...
He doesn't understand the word 'envelope'...
He's scared of bells...
He's terrified of ducks...
He sucks the moisture from ducks...
He knows two facts about ducks, and both of them are wrong...
All we know is, he's called the Stig!

---

*   We realise some of these contradict each other. It just goes to show
how little we *really* know about our tame racing driver.

Can a Car Beat a...?

S = Series   E = Episode

EPISODE	CAR	DRIVER	OPPONENT	COURSE	WINNER
S1E9	Radical SR3	Hammond	Aerobatic Plane	TG track	Plane
S3E3	Saab 9-5	The Stig	Harrier Jump Jet	TG track	Plane
S4E1	Aston Martin DB9	Clarkson	French TGV train	TG track to Monaco	**The car!**
S4E4	Ford SportKa	May	Racing Pigeons	Cotswolds to Mansfield	Pigeons
S4E4	Mercedes-Benz SL500	The Stig	Ronnie O'Sullivan and fourteen snooker balls	TG track	O'Sullivan
S5E2	Mitsubishi Evo VII	Ben Collins	All-terrain skateboarder	A hill	Skateboarder
S5E2	Bowler Wildcat	Ben Collins	All-terrain skateboarder	The same hill	**The car!**
S5E8	Mitsubishi Evo rally car	Henning Solberg & May	Norwegian Olympic bobsleigh team & Hammond	Lillehammer bobsleigh track	Bobsleigh
S5E8	Ferrari 612 Scaglietti	Clarkson	Aerolane	TG studio to Switzerland	**The car!**
S6E1	Range Rover Sport	Clarkson	Challenger Tank	A firing range in Dorset	Tank
S6E6	Mercedes-Benz SLR McLaren	Clarkson	Ferry	Heathrow to Oslo	**The car!**
S6E7	Fiat Nuova Panda	Clarkson	Marathon runner	London Marathon course, in rush hour	Runner
S6E10	Modified off-road vehicle	Hammond	Snowmobile	A lake in Iceland	Snowmobile
S7E2	Audi RS4	Clarkson	Rock climbers	A mountain gorge in France	Climbers
S7E4	Renault Clio III	May	Downhill bike racer	Lisbon, Portugal	Bike
S7E5	Bugatti Veyron	Clarkson	Light aircraft (flown by May)	Alba, Italy to London	**The car!**
S7E6	Mazda MX-5	Hammond	Greyhound	Shelbourne Park in Dublin	Greyhound

36

Winter Olympics	Jaguar XK8	Clarkson	Speed skater	Ice rink	Skater
S8E2	Tomcat 4x4	Hammond	Kayak with an outboard motor	A lake in Iceland	Kayak
S8E4	Porsche Cayenne Turbo S	Hammond	British army parachutist	Cyprus	Parachutist
S8E7	Peugeot 207	May	Two parkour runners	Liverpool	Runners
Polar Special	Toyota Hilux	Clarkson & May	Dogsled & Hammond	Resolute, Canada to magnetic North Pole	The car!
S10E3	Bugatti Veyron	Hammond	Eurofighter Typhoon	An airfield	Plane
S10E5	Mercedes-Benz GL	May	Public transport, a bike and a boat	Kew Bridge to City Airport	Bike
S10E5	Aston Martin V8 Vantage	Hammond	Rocket-powered rollerskater	TG track	Skater
S10E6	Alfa Romeo 159	May	A tall man in a wetsuit	Humber River	Tall man
S10E9	Fiat Nuova 500	May	Two BMX bikers	Budapest, Hungary	Cyclists
S11E2	Audi RS6 estate	Hammond	Two skiers	Les Arcs, France	Skiers
S11E4	Nissan GT-R	Clarkson	Japanese Bullet Train	Across Japan	The car!
S11E5	Daihatsu Terios	Clarkson	Hammond and hunters on horseback	Fields in Gloucester	Hunters
S12E5	Ferrari Daytona	Hammond	XSR 48 powerboat	Mediterranean coast	Boat
S13E1	Jaguar XK120	May	New steam train (Clarkson) and an old motorbike (Hammond)	London to Edinburgh	The car!
S13E4	Porsche Panamera	Hammond and May	A letter (and Royal Mail)	The length of Britain (Scillies to Orkneys)	Letter
S13E4	Mitsubishi Evo VII	Clarkson	British Army vehicles	A firing range in Dorset	Army
S15E5	VW Touareg	Hammond	Two snowmobiles	A ski resort in Sweden	THE CAR!
S16E01	Porsche 911	Hammond	VW Beetle dropped from a helicopter	South African desert	Beetle

Cars that Jeremy has Broken

- **Mercedes-Benz S-Class:** failed to get round to driving it, because he couldn't get it to accept a phone number via voice-recognition.
- **Vauxhall Signum:** Tied string and poles to the wheel and pedals so he could drive it from the back seat.
- **Saab 9-5 Aero:** knackered the tyres.

- An old **Mercedes-Benz S-Class**, which he utterly ruined by fitting flagstones and wooden floorboards, a wingback armchair, a wood-burning stove, a bookcase with a globe, potted plants and a lampshade, coffee table, curtains and leaded windows. 'Do you know what?' 'What?' 'This is terrible.'
- His ropey old **Camaro** he bought in America, when he put a cow on the roof. He didn't break it, but he made it smell pretty horrible. He also sabotaged James's **Cadillac** with a spatula.

- The stretch limo he built from a **Fiat Panda** – it snapped in two.

- The arctic **Toyota** – by losing patience and trying to drive through ice, he knackered the propshaft, the auxiliary fuel tank and a shock absorber. He also knocked one tyre off its rim, but the Icelanders managed to fix that... by setting fire to it.

- The **Lancia Beta** he bought in Botswana; it was pretty rubbish to start with, and after he took the doors, seats and windows off, it looked considerably worse.

- The **BMW 330d** repmobile they filled with their own eco-diesel and raced for twenty-four hours – though, to be fair, Richard and James did their fair share of breaking this one.

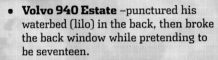

- **Bentley Brooklands** – it had so much torque he managed to shred one of the tyres
- **Renault Magnum truck** – set fire to the trailer.

- **Volvo 940 Estate** –punctured his waterbed (lilo) in the back, then broke the back window while pretending to be seventeen.

- **Mitsubishi Evo VII** – got caught by the Army, who shot it to pieces.
- Richard's **Nissan 300ZX** on the way to the French ice race – he chucked part of the roof off a cliff.

- **Renault Twingo** – deliberately crashed it to demonstrate how cheap spares were, then drove it off a pier into the sea while trying to catch a ferry.

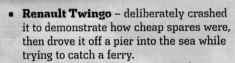

- **BMW 'art car'** that he dumped in a ditch on the way to Middlesborough.
- **Reliant Robin** – rolled it repeatedly and ended up in a canal.

It's not all bad, though – in France, Jeremy actually managed to fix a broken bulb. Which, for the world's most impractical man, is quite a feat.

I **MENDED** SOMETHING!

Cars That Have Injured Jeremy

Top Gear's favourite shouty tall man has suffered many hideous injuries while selflessly testing cars.* Here are four of the worst...

Vehicle: Nissan GT-R

Aargh! My neck's just **gone!**

Year: 2008
Injury: Cricked neck
Reason for injury: Taking corners too fast on the Fuji race track in Japan and having a huge head.

Vehicle: Volvo 760

Year: 2004
Injury: Broken thumb
Reason for injury: Driving into a solid wall at 40mph, when instructed to do so at 30mph.

Your thumb's **broken!**

No it's not. It's just chipped.

* Kids, don't try this at home

40

Vehicle: Prodrive P2

Year: 2006
Injury: Motion sickness
Reason for injury: Driving round in circles too quickly, eating too much lunch.

BLEEURGH!

Vehicle: Renault Magnum lorry

Year: 2008
Injury: Bruised neck, back and fingers
Reason for injury: Crashing into a brick wall at 56mph.

Strewth, that **really** hurts! Ah, ah, aah, aaah...

CRASH

Britain versus Australia

The British Top Gear team thrashed their Aussie rivals in a completely fair contest this year. But how do the two nations match up in the cold hard world of statistics? Let's find out.

NB: We definitely didn't choose the categories just so Britain could win. We wouldn't do something like that.

	Britain	**Australia**
Number of F1 world champions	**10** (Jackie Stewart, Jim Clark, Graham Hill, Mike Hawthorn, John Surtees, James Hunt, Nigel Mansell, Damon Hill, Lewis Hamilton, Jenson Button)	2 (Jack Brabham, Alan Jones)
Total number of F1 championships	**14**	4
Number of World Rally Champions	**2** (Colin McRae, Richard Burns)	0
Speed limit	**70mph**	68mph
Best-selling car	**Ford Fiesta** (Yes, the Commodore is a cool car, but has it ever been used in a beach landing with a squadron of Royal Marines? Thought not)	Holden Commodore
Fastest-accelerating production car	**Ariel Atom V8**, 0-62mph in 2.5 seconds	HSV W427, 0-62mph in 4.7 seconds
Number of miles of paved road:	247,000	**567,000** (but most of them are straight and boring)
Most expensive car	**Aston Martin One-77**: £1,300,000	HSV W127: £90,000
Number of Ashes series won (it's cricket, so it doesn't really count)	30 (but we've won three of the last four! Doesn't that count for something? No?)	**31**
Number of Olympic gold medals	**207**	131
Height of tallest presenter	**6'5"** (Jeremy Clarkson)	6'1" (Shane Jacobson)
Number of football World Cups won	**1** (1966)	0
FINAL SCORES	**10**	**2**

VERDICT: Another crushing victory for the Brits. It's just getting too easy to beat the Aussies nowadays...

What Stuff can you Turn into Fuel?

In 2007, the boys went twenty-four-hour racing in a BMW powered by diesel brewed from their own harvest of rapeseed. But what else can real scientists turn into fuel?

Beer

American brewer Sierra Nevada turns its 1.6 million gallons of leftover beer yeast into bioethanol – that's the fuel that the Koenigsegg CCXR runs on!

Cow poo

Scientists have discovered how to generate ethanol – a powerful alcohol-based fuel – from cow dung. Good news: ethanol gives cars even more power than super-unleaded petrol!

Jatropha

The seeds from this scrubby plant can be turned into biodiesel. Luckily, jatropha can grow in bad soil, so it doesn't have to take up valuable farmland dedicated to important things like sugar, fruit and racetracks...

Human waste

Or 'poo', as it's better known. In 2009, a British company showed off a VW Beetle that ran on methane gas produced by fermented human waste. Don't worry, they say it doesn't smell at all!

Plastic bottles

A French company recently announced plans to open ten recycling plants in the UK, each able to turn waste plastic – including bottles, carrier bags and yoghurt pots – into delicious diesel…

Koenigsegg CCXR – the supergreen supercar

Hat Tricks

A hat says a lot about a man. Sadly, in most of these pictures, it says 'I look like an idiot.' Tick off all the ones you've seen.

What Historical Events Happened on the Presenters' Birthdays?

16 January

1759 The British Museum opens

1853 Andre Michelin (yes, the tyre bloke), born

1901 Frank Zamboni, inventor of the ice-rink resurfacing vehicle, born

1909 Ernest Shackleton's expedition reaches the South Pole

1948 John Carpenter, film director, born

1959 Sade, singer (ask your dad), born

1963 James Daniel May born

1967 Robert J. Van de Graaff, nuclear physicist and inventor of the Van de Graaff Generator, dies

1974 Kate Moss, model, born

1979 Aaliyah, R&B singer, born

1981 Bernard Lee, actor (M in the first eleven Bond films), dies

1981 Bobby Zamora, footballer, born

1991 The US begins the first Gulf War with Iraq

1996 Kaye Webb, publisher of Puffin Books, dies

11 April

1689 William III and Mary II are crowned king and queen of Britain

1775 The last execution for witchcraft in Germany

1865 Abraham Lincoln makes his last public speech

1890 Joseph Merrick, 'the Elephant Man', dies

1905 Albert Einstein reveals his Theory of Relativity

1960 Jeremy Charles Robert Clarkson born

1966 Lisa Stansfield, singer, born

1969 Cerys Matthews, singer, born

1970 *Apollo 13* is launched

1976 The first Apple computer is demonstrated

1985 Enver Hoxha, Albanian Communist dictator, dies

1987 Joss Stone, singer, born

1992 Disneyland Paris opens

1994 Dakota Blue Richards, actress, born

19 December

1154   Henry II crowned at Westminster Abbey

1843   Charles Dickens publishes *A Christmas Carol*

1848   Emily Brontë, author, dies

1924   The last Rolls-Royce Silver Ghost is sold in London

1932   The BBC World Service begins broadcasting

1958   Limahl, singer with Kajagoogoo (ask your mum), born

1962   The first satnav satellite is launched

1969   Richard Mark Hammond born

1972   *Apollo 17* returns to Earth

1974   Ricky Ponting, cricketer, born

1980   Jake Gyllenhaal, actor, born

1983   The Jules Rimet World Cup Trophy is stolen in Brazil

1985   Lady Sovereign, rapper, born

1999   Desmond Llewelyn, actor (Q in the Bond films), dies

How to Say the Name of the Volcano James Drove Up

Eyjafjallajökull

Ey-a-fyah-**LAY**-okkle.

How Does Satnav Work?

Satnav. You stick a little box on the dashboard and it knows where you are, AND how to get to where you want to go. Amazing, if you think about it – but how does it work?

1 Out of sight in orbit around Earth are twenty-four satellites called the Global Positioning System, GPS. They each transmit a radio message every thirty seconds* saying:
- Which satellite they are
- Where they are in relation to Earth
- What time each message is sent
- Which satellites are working properly

2 Your GPS receiver, or satnav, picks up these radio messages all the time. It contains a clock, so it can count how long each message takes to reach it. Radio signals always travel at the same speed, so the satnav can then work out how far away it is from each satellite.

---

* The same satellites also transmit much faster, more accurate signals that can only be used by the military. GPS belongs to the US armed forces, and they can turn it off any time they feel like it. Without telling the rest of us.

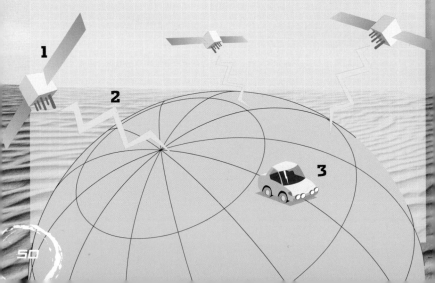

3 If your satnav can receive a good signal from four or more different satellites, then it can work out its position pretty accurately, and also check that its clock is right. If it can only 'see' three satellites, it can make a pretty good guess. The position is worked out as often as it gets new messages.*

Let's have a **satnav** challenge. Becuase mine is German, and will be **superior**.

Good idea. First to get to the People's Palace is the **winner**.

How can it not have... the Italians don't acknowledge the **existence** of Romania!

4 The second part of satnav in cars is a stored map. This needs to be accurate and up-to-date – and include the country you happen to be in. It also helps if it knows things like the height of bridges and the width of minor roads.

5 The final part is software to calculate routes, store journeys and give instructions in a really annoying voice. Route planning in the UK often depends on postcodes, which aren't always accurate; a church or a campsite may not have a letterbox, so it won't have a postcode. And your satnav may not know the nifty shortcuts, so it can't always beat the old-fashioned, pre-satnav method – **Knowing Where You're Going**.

Please-follow-the-road

I will **gladly** follow the road. Technology and I are getting on absolutely **fine**.

Calling-Steve-Accountant

I saw it first!

No, **I** saw it first!

No no no, **don't** do that!

---

* Usually every five seconds, but could be as long as thirty seconds. Which at 70mph, means you'd have moved 900 metres without knowing where you are.

How to be a Limousine Chauffeur

In 2008, the boys proved themselves to be rubbish chauffeurs when they tried to get Lemar, Jamelia and Chris Moyles to the Brit Awards in their home-made limos. Here's how to be a proper chauffeur.

Look smart

White shirt, collar, black tie and black shoes should be worn at all times. Brown leather gloves should be worn while driving.

Where are we now?

We're just coming on to... um... err... erm...

Know the local area

Your client will appreciate it if you are able to offer handy tips on good places to eat or visit. However...

That's the intercom, you press that if you want to speak to me. Don't use it if it starts to rain, you'll get **electrocuted.**

Only speak when spoken to

Do not enter into a conversation with your passenger unless they initiate it.

Thank you!

Drive safely and calmly

Anticipate the road to make the journey as comfortable as possible for your passenger. No violent stops or Jeremy-style cornering!

Be respectful

Touch your cap when opening the door to allow your passenger in or out the car. Never allow your passenger to open the door themselves.

Don't rush

Wait until all your passengers are comfortably seated before strapping into the driver's seat.

Be neat and tidy

Keep your car perfectly clean, inside and out.

And, most importantly...

Don't get horribly lost in London and deliver your VIP guest to the Brit Awards two hours late!

Sorry Chris.

Sorry about the ladder thing. The steps weren't ideal.

Some Say...
(again)...

For some reason he's allergic to the Dutch...
He has no understanding of clouds...
He appears on high value stamps in Sweden...
He's wanted by the CIA...
He can catch fish with his tongue...
He's been banned from the Chelsea Flower Show...
He's banned from the town of Chichester...
There are seventeen different reasons why he's
    banned from the Northampton branch of
    Little Chef...
There's an airport in Russia named after him...
Wherever you are in the world if you tune your radio
    to 88.4 you can actually hear his thoughts...
If he caught fire he'd burn for a thousand days...
He can swim seven lengths underwater...
He invented Branston Pickle...
He invented November...
He invented the curtain...
He isn't machine washable...
All his potted plants are called Steve...
He thought *Star Wars* was a documentary...
When he slows down, brake lights come on in his buttocks...
It's impossible for him to wear socks...
He has twelve GCSEs, all in Domestic Science...
On Thursdays he becomes incredibly bulbous...
Recently, pigs in Mexico started to die of something called 'Stigflu'...
He has some terrible plans involving the moon...
If he felt like it, he could fire Alan Sugar...
If he could be bothered he could crack the Da Vinci code in forty-three
    seconds...
He was turned down for a place on *I'm a Celebrity* because he is one...
His new Christmas range of fragrances includes the great smell
    of Wednesday...
The drinks cabinet in his car contains fourteen different types
    of custard...

...all we know is, he's called the Stig!

55

Supercars in which Jeremy has Beaten Richard and James

Jeremy proudly boasts that, in a supercar, he can beat James and Richard... no matter what form of transport they choose! Here are the big races he has won – with the help of some seriously fast cars....

Aston Martin DB9 vs train

From Surrey to Monaco, on France's Mediterranean coast. James and Richard took the Eurostar and France's high-speed train, but Jeremy defeated them in the big Aston.

Ferrari 612 vs plane

From Surrey to Verbier, a ski resort in Switzerland. Hammond and May got public transport to Heathrow airport, a plane to Geneva, and then a train and coach... but still lost.

McLaren-Mercedes SLR vs ferry

From Heathrow to Oslo, in Norway. Jeremy drove 1,320 miles through Europe while Richard and James took a plane to Newcastle and then a ferry to Norway. If their speedboat hadn't broken, would they have won? Probably not.

Oh my god. I've just turned the **satnav** off!

Nissan GT-R vs Bullet Train

From Hakui to Mount Nokogiri. Japan has one of the fastest, most efficient public transport systems in the world, but it was no match for the four-wheel drive supercar... even though Jeremy couldn't understand the satnav!

Bugatti Veyron vs plane

From Alba in Italy to Central London. Jeremy had the world's most powerful car, but Captain Slow had a private plane. However, he wasn't allowed to fly it at night, so James and Richard finished their journey by train. They lost by seconds.

Ways to Upspec your Car

I love this whole modifying thing, it's **brilliant**.

Jeremy's right. What's not to love? You will never be able to afford a supercar – so buy something cheap and then 'mod' it to make it look (and go) better.

There are two routes to take: styling (to change the appearance) and tuning (to change the performance). Some mods do both – spoilers and low-profile tyres, for instance. The only decision to make is how much you want to spend. Richard and James met a chap who'd spent £26,000 on his Peugeot 306, adding three TVs, a PlayStation, huge speakers, a 3 litre V6 engine, scissor doors, adjustable suspension, rearview camera...

Styling options

- Body panels in any shape you fancy
- Add spoilers, wings, skirts and sills
- New headlights or other lights added anywhere (neon underneath, mmm)
- Tinted windows
- Wheels, tyres, hubcaps and wheelnuts
- Add chrome trim, or take off the badges and even the locks
- Grilles, vents and exhausts in any size you like

- Change the doors to scissors or gullwing – or weld them shut
- Make the engine all shiny (that's the technical term)
- Wild new paint colour, sprayed art or vinyl stickers
- Fancy racing steering wheel
- Dashboard and instruments
- Upholstery, carpets and seats
- Sound system – you can fit forty or more speakers in a hatchback
- Games console, TV, fridge, heaters
- Lower the suspension, or make it dance around
- Roll bars and racing seatbelts

Tuning options

- Reprogram the electronic control unit (ECU) to make the engine work better
- Swap the engine completely
- Add a supercharger or turbocharger

- Add **nitrous**. A kit that squirts nitrous oxide (NOS) into an engine makes it more powerful somehow (but it can damage the engine)

- Take away the heavy bits. Lighter cars go faster – remember the Ariel Atom?
- Put a spoiler on a rear-wheel drive car to help push the tyres down on to the road, giving better grip
  A splitter will do the same for a front-wheel drive car
- Fiddle with the engine in complicated ways that only James understands

Remember though – the best modding in the world won't turn a Renault Avantime into a Mitsubishi Evo X. As Jeremy and the chaps proved.

Mitsubishi Evo X

Not a Mitsubishi Evo X

What to Get Around on until You're Old Enough to Drive

You can ride bikes, scooters, dodgems and karts – which can all be pretty exciting. But what about the good stuff – with motors?

Actually, you can drive anything you like, however old you are – BUT it has to be on **private land** (which the public can't access) AND with the **owner's permission**. So no supermarket car parks, or some field off the ring road. Some racetracks will let you have a go, if a grown-up gets the vehicle there – there are junior stockcar races, for instance.

ArgoCat (on private land)

Racing quad bikes

If you work for a farmer, you can drive a **tractor** or a registered agricultural **quad bike** on his land. And at sixteen, you can take a tractor test so you can drive it from one field to the next on the road.

You can also ride a **moped** at sixteen, if you pass a test and get a valid provisional driving licence first. A moped has a top speed of 50kph (31mph) and a maximum engine size of 50cc. Wahey.

And at seventeen, you can drive a **proper car**. On the proper road. First you need a provisional licence (which you can apply for when you're sixteen). You also need a taxed, road-legal car, and someone to sit next to you who's over twenty-one and has had a full licence for at least three years. (That could be your dad, but it's probably better if it was a driving instructor.) You can take your test on your seventeenth birthday, though that may be a bit ambitious.

Hovercrafts

However, don't expect to actually have your own car unless you win the lottery. As Jeremy, Richard and James found out, it is *incredibly* expensive to insure any car when you are seventeen.*

This is because the insurance companies are rather confident you will have a terrible accident almost instantly. As Jeremy found out: 'You can imagine my surprise when [thirty-six hours after passing my driving test] I found myself in a field...

Electric toy cars

Jeremy pretending to be a 17-year-old driver

surrounded by bits of what **used** to be my mum's Audi. How did this happen? I'm the *best driver in the world*, and I've gone and stuffed it!'

Tractor

---

* Don't think you can get round this by riding some natty electric bike or skateboard with a little motor. You need a proper licence and insurance to take these on the road, just like a car.

Toyotas – the Toughest Cars Ever?

Top Gear loves Toyota trucks. They've used – and abused – them several times, in a variety of interesting ways.

Kill it!

Spend £1000 on a thirteen-year-old Toyota Hilux diesel, with 190,000 miles on the clock and which looked like only ten of them were left on the road.

Then... drive it down some steps; scrape it against a wall; run it into a tree; scrape it against another wall; drown it in the Bristol Channel, filling it with sand and salty water; drop it; drive it through a shed; drop a Mistral GT caravan on it; hit it with a huge metal demolition ball; set fire to it; put it 240ft up on top of Rachel Point tower block in Hackney... and demolish the building.

And after all that, it not only starts, it actually moves. Incredible.

Float it!

Jeremy wanted to make a simple amphibious car. 'Why not just get a car, and then put an outboard motor on the back?' Which made the Toyota Hilux ideal for the job, in his opinion. He wasn't allowed to put 450hp outboards on the back, and bodged the waterproofing a bit. But it worked... kind of. The Toybota proved to be a pig to handle at speed (which was the only way Jeremy would drive it). He flipped and sank it within inches of the finish. Nothing wrong with the Toybota, mind – just the driver.

Freeze it!

What do you use to drive to
the North Pole? Obviously,
a Toyota. All you have to do is give it to some Icelandic mechanics
to tweak it a bit. Add some enormous handmade £2,500 wheels, move the
suspension forwards so the doors will open, give it heavy duty diffs and
suspension, a thick sump guard, pointless headlamps (Jeremy wanted
them but it doesn't get dark up there in the summer), marine satnav and a
long-distance fuel tank filled with a freeze-resistant mixture of diesel and
avgas. And a gun. Despite Jeremy and James' best efforts at sinking and
crashing the Toyota, it made it. Of course.

Burn it!

There was a spare Toyota from the trip to the Pole (which the camera
crew had driven). Rather than waste it, James went to Iceland to resurrect
it. He added a corrugated iron roof (for the falling lava) and a special
wheel-cooling system (to stop the tyres melting). This contained vodka
to stop it freezing. After a scary night drive in a terrible storm, James
headed up the slopes of a real live volcano, armed with a bucket and a
garden trowel on a stick. When the fresh lumps of lava started banging
on the roof, he bravely stopped to scoop up a chunk. He stayed still long
enough to set fire to a wheel, so it was time to leg it. Yet again, the Toyota
did the business.

Brilliant Bonneville

In 2008, the boys travelled to Bonneville Salt Flats in the USA to set some speed records in their American cars. But why is Bonneville such a legendary location for petrolheads?

- Bonneville Salt Flats is a salt pan in the western state of Utah.

- It formed many thousands of years ago when a huge saltwater lake evaporated during a hot spell in Earth's history.

- This left a flat basin covered in a layer of salt almost five feet deep.

- The huge area of the salt pan and its smooth surface make it perfect for speed records.

968 BONNEVILLE SALT FLATS—WORLD'S FASTEST SPEEDWAY—NEAR GREAT SALT LAKE, UTAH

PHOTO COURTESY BILL SHIPLER, SALT LAKE

SIR MALCOLM CAMPBELL IN THE "BLUEBIRD" DOING OVER 301 MILES PER HOUR   7A-H517

- Bonneville was first used for motorsports in 1912, but achieved worldwide fame in 1935 when British racer Malcolm Campbell set a land speed record of 301mph in his 'Blue Bird' car, powered by a Rolls-Royce engine.

- Since then, ten land speed records have been set at Bonneville. The fastest speed reached was in 1970, when Gary Gabelich hit 622mph in his rocket-powered 'Blue Flame'.

- British pilot Andy Green, who was the first man to break the sound barrier in a car, also set a speed record for diesel cars when he achieved 350mph in the JCB Dieselmax at Bonneville in 2006.

- Jeremy Clarkson set a new speed record for production cars when he hit 176mph in his Corvette ZR1 on the boys' American road trip.

What was British Leyland?

In 2007, the boys set out to prove that British Leyland made some good cars. They failed, mainly. But what was British Leyland, and why isn't it around today?

British Leyland was formed in 1968. It brought together almost every major British car maker – including Jaguar, Rover and MG – into one huge company, aiming to compete with giant American manufacturers like General Motors.

Old men with hammers!

At its peak, British Leyland employed quarter of a million workers and built millions of cars each year.

Unfortunately, many of the cars built by British Leyland companies had been in production for almost twenty years. They were out of date, but there were no plans to replace them.

Breakdowns!

British Leyland bosses rushed a bunch of new cars into production, including *Top Gear*'s favourite classic, the Morris Marina. Because these cars were built in a hurry, they proved to be unreliable, leaky rustbuckets.

Strikes!

Worse was to follow. In the 1970s, Britain was hit by an energy crisis, meaning British Leyland factories could only open for three days a week. Many workers also went on strike, which led to British Leyland going bankrupt in 1975.

British Leyland continued to produce cars in the late 1970s and 1980s, including Jeremy's favourite, the Rover SD1. But many of its factories had to close and it began to kill off or sell the brands it had brought together in the 1960s.

Bits falling off!

Leaks!

In 1984, Jaguar was sold to Ford, and in 1988 BMW bought Rover. Over the next few years, the brands within British Leyland were all either shut down or sold abroad. Almost all of the factories were closed, and today there are few reminders of the sad history of one of Britain's biggest companies.

BRITISH
LEYLAND
a British Leyland presentation

Damp!

Rubble!

Ten Amphibious Cars

Jeremy, James and Richard are well-practised at turning road cars into water-based transport. But how do their amphibious cars stack up against the best in the business?

DUKW

This six-wheeled military truck was used by the British in the Second World War to land on shorelines without ports. It was widely known as 'The Duck'.

Schwimmwagen

The German's answer to the Duck, the name of this pram-like creation literally means 'swim-car'. Based on the Volkswagen Beetle, it was designed by the man behind many of Porsche's most beautiful cars.

Amphicar

About 4,000 of these leaky monstrosities were sold to members of the public between 1961 and 1968. Most of them sank. Oars were issued as standard.

Gibbs Aquada

Virgin millionaire Richard Branson piloted this high-speed amphibian across the English Channel in 2004. His journey took just 100 minutes, setting a record that *Top Gear* completely failed to beat.

Rinspeed Splash

The Swiss-built Splash was designed to 'skim' over the surface of the water on the clever blades mounted on its underside. It could do 125mph on dry land, which was probably the best place for it.

Panda Terramere 4

What do you get when you stick a rubber ring onto a Fiat Panda? One of the slowest amphibious cars ever! The Terramere took a full six hours to cross the English Channel in 2006.

Hydra Spyder

It's an idea straight from the Jeremy Clarkson School of Thought: wedging the V8 engine from a Corvette into a floating supercar. Just one snag: the Spyder costs £85,000. Ouch.

Toybota Hilux

Jeremy's brave invention was perfect but for one tiny flaw: the fact it preferred to be upside down. It nearly beat May's Triumph sailboat, but fell at the very last hurdle.

The Dampervan

Volkswagen camper vans aren't traditionally the best at keeping the water out on dry land. As Richard discovered in soggy fashion, they don't fare any better in reservoirs.

The Mayflower

Always a man of traditional engineering, James decided to embrace the natural power of wind to gain victory in the boy's first amphibious car challenge. Slow and steady wins the race...

Eating in the Car – Rights and Wrongs

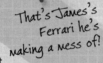

> These chocolate bars just go **everywhere**.

YES!

- **Fruit**, especially prepared fruit in a bag or box so there's no peel, pips or stones
- **Water** or juice in a bottle with a spill-proof cap
- **Dried fruit bars** or flapjacks – sticky enough to hold together and not leave crumbs
- **Dried meat**, like biltong or beef jerky
- Sucky or chewy **sweets**
- A **sandwich** with a sticky filling that won't fall out
- **Crisps** you can fit in your mouth in one go
- **Wipes**
- A **bag** for rubbish

That's James's Ferrari he's making a mess of!

NO!

- **Chocolate** – bits fall off and melt in your lap
- **Milk** – probably the worst thing you could have in a car. It soaks into the upholstery, then turns to cheese. Once you've spilt milk in a car, you'll have to sell it to someone with no nose
- **Hot drinks**, unless you're parked – too easy to spill them in your lap
- **Cheesy snacks** that turn your fingers orange
- **Cornish pasties** or sausage rolls – flaky bits of pastry end up everywhere
- **Cartons of drink** with a little straw – either you squirt it around the car when you open it, or leave the last bit which leaks out on the floor
- **Burgers** or **fried chicken** – hot, sticky, greasy and comes in paper bags that break. Plenty of reasons to not be lovin' it
- **Cans of pop** – if they get a bit warm and shaken up (and they will), the cans will spray everywhere when you open them
- **Biscuits** – guess where the crumbs end up
- **Roadkill** – you're not allowed to eat anything you run over. However if *someone else* runs it over, you can. But you probably still shouldn't!

That is a **cow** on your Camaro.

Oops!

71

Supercar Fuel Economy

In these tricky times, it's important to know which is the most fuel-efficient supercar. So put one gallon of fuel in each car and press the go pedal. Which one will run out of juice first?

Supercars going flat out:

Ferrari 599

Aston Martin DBS

Mercedes-Benz McLaren SLR

Lamborghini Murcielago

Audi R8

If you don't rag it, things get a bit better:

Ferrari Enzo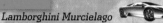

Maserati MC12

Bugatti Veyron

Koenigsegg

Gumpert Apollo

Can a supergreen ecomobile do any better?

Prius going flat-out

BMW M3 following the Prius
Which shows that it's not necessarily *what* you drive, but *how* you drive.

But if you want real fuel economy:

Toyota Aygo or Peugeot 107
Or if you can stand a diesel:

Renault Clio or Citroen C2 diesel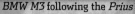

| 10mpg | 20mpg |

Motorbikes, According to Jeremy

Jeremy would rather hop 1000 miles to Hanoi than ride the scooter he was told to buy. He swore at it, fell off it, had it fixed again and again (one time, with a plastic bag full of weeds), kicked it and generally hated it. (He did like Vietnam though.)

Look around us, what do you see everywhere?

No. I can't. You **know** I can't do that.

What else is there? I bet you can buy a bike for that.

You can buy a lump of excrement for that, but it doesn't mean I'm going to.

Look, it's transport with an engine, it's the **only** choice.

I can't do that. Guys, I can't do that. I can't ride a bike. I'm sorry, this is stupid. It's a thousand miles in the rainy season in a country with not very good roads, and **I can't ride a bike!**

The reason I don't ride a motorcycle is because I have a **large brain**. The reason why crash helmets are **small** is because people who wear them haven't got a brain. Otherwise they'd have a **car**.

74

Oh **BEEP**. This is terrifying! There are just bikes absolutely **everywhere**. Oh my God, one's stalled right in front of me. This is the **only** motorbike I've ever had, and it is **undriveable**.

I am the most **miserable** person alive!

I'm a member of the club now. **Don't** like it, **hate** biking, it's a **stupid** idea.

After his first bike accident

Get out of the way bikers! Get a **car** and some proper clothes for God's sake!

At the Nürburgring

One in four fatal or serious accidents on an A road involves a bike. Now there are only **eight** bikes on the road in Britain, and they're involved in a **quarter** of all crashes! In terms of miles covered, they're more dangerous than **puff adders**.

How do Self-Driving Cars Work?

In 2007, Jeremy got a hands-free hot lap of the TG test track in a self-driving BMW. These cars might be the future of transport, but how do they work?

Magic motors

First, a car needs to be able to control the steering, accelerator and brakes. This is usually done by attaching a number of motors to the controls.

I can't **believe** I'm going to do this.

Nifty navigation

Next, a car needs to know where it is. For this, it will use GPS – the same system found in the satellite navigation devices of modern cars, which receives information from a number of satellites in space to determine its exact position.

It's coming to the first corner. Brake please – **BRAKE!**

Look, his feet aren't on the pedals!

Special sensors

A self-driving car also needs to know what is around it. For this, it uses a system of sensors, including radar and laser beams. If it detects something in front of it, the car will brake hard to avoid an accident.

Stig, you are sacked. You are **so** sacked!

Clever computers

The car needs a huge 'brain' to process all this information. Self-driving cars use some of the most powerful computers available – and all to perform a task that most humans can achieve while singing along to the radio!

95mph through the tyres! **Please** don't get it wrong!

Now how do I **stop** it? I forgot to ask the man how I stop it.

How to Drive on Ice

In their cheap rear-wheel drive cars in the Alps, the Top Gear boys proved themselves very bad at driving on ice. Here's how the experts do it safely...

It's **easy**, gentleness is the – oh no!

Avoid aggressive movements

Don't jerk the steering wheel, slam on the brakes or mash the accelerator pedal, as this will send your car into a spin.

It's like an **accident** in slow motion.

Start off in second gear

Trying to pull away in first gear will often result in your wheels spinning but your car going nowhere. If you can't move, try second gear instead, but be gentle with the clutch!

We're being **humiliated!** You cheese-eating sideways monkeys!

Use the engine to slow the car

When heading down a hill, put the car into a low gear and use the braking effect of the engine to slow the car. This is less likely to result in a skid than if you hit the brakes.

How do they **do** that?

Use winter tyres

The tyres on most British cars aren't suitable for driving on snow or icy roads. Proper winter tyres – as most locals use in Canada and the Alps – give much more grip and control.

Steer into a slide

If your car starts to skid, you need to 'steer into it'. This means that, if the rear of your car starts to slide to the left, you should turn the wheel to the left to stop the skid and regain control. But remember: no sudden movements, and don't hit the brakes!

The **best** rear-wheel drive car money can buy is the **Morris Marina.**

It's the flag! Surely not – not the **Marina!**

79

The Greatest F1 Drivers

In 2009, the Stig removed his helmet to reveal...
Michael Schumacher, the most successful F1 driver
in history. But how do the German's seven world titles
stack up against the sport's greatest champions?

Michael Stigmacher

Ayrton Senna

Driver	Country	Number of championships	Year of first championship	Year of last championship
Michael Schumacher	Germany	7	1994	2004
Juan Manuel Fangio	Argentina	5	1951	1957
Alain Prost	France	4	1985	1993
Jack Brabham	Australia	3	1959	1966
Jackie Stewart	Britain	3	1969	1973
Niki Lauda	Austria	3	1975	1984
Nelson Piquet	Brazil	3	1981	1987
Ayrton Senna	Brazil	3	1988	1991

Juan Manuel Fangio

Jack Brabham

Niki Lauda

Jackie Stewart

Nelson Piquet

Alain Prost

The Bugatti Veyron

If you've got a million pounds sitting around doing nothing (and if you can persuade the people at Bugatti to take you on as a customer), why not buy a Veyron?

You can go and watch your car being built in Molsheim, France, in an oval workshop the same shape as the Bugatti logo. Eight craftsmen assemble each car by hand, taking almost three weeks to put the 3,700 parts together. They only finish one or two a week, so there are only about 400 in the world.

Want a convertible version? OK. Want one made of carbon fibre and titanium? No problem. And when your car is ready, you know you've got one of the most incredible cars in the world.

- The heart of the beast is an 8-litre W16 engine, producing over 1000hp and capable of pushing the car to over 400kph.

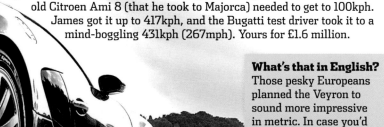

- Every single part is made of the lightest material possible – magnesium, titanium, aluminium or carbon fibre, depending on what works best.
- The automatic seven-speed gearbox changes gear in a sixth of a second – that's faster than you can blink.
- If you plan to go over 375kph, you have to press a special button before you even set off, so the car adjusts into the perfect shape to go superfast.
- The wing on the back can angle up to make the car 350kg heavier, so it grips the road harder, or flip right up to help the brakes. This means it can brake from 100kph to a standstill in 2.3 seconds. The carbon ceramic brakes may get red hot, but they can cope: they're safe up to 1,100°C, which can melt copper.
- As soon as the car's three computers think something's about to go wrong, they contact Bugatti to warn them. And Bugatti can find out where every one of their cars is, thanks to built-in GPS.
- It only has two airbags; it doesn't need any more, because the body of the car forms a safety cage that's as safe as an F1 racing car.

If that's not special enough for you, the clever chaps at Bugatti looked at the Veyron and thought, 'You know what? That's not fast enough.' Say hello to the Bugatti Veyron Super Sport. Bigger turbos and intercoolers help the engine pump out 1,200hp. The body is all carbon-fibre to save more weight, and the shape is tweaked to make it slip through the air like a greased weasel. So this Veyron can get to 400kph in 32s – what James's old Citroen Ami 8 (that he took to Majorca) needed to get to 100kph. James got it up to 417kph, and the Bugatti test driver took it to a mind-boggling 431kph (267mph). Yours for £1.6 million.

What's that in English?
Those pesky Europeans planned the Veyron to sound more impressive in metric. In case you'd forgotten:
100kph = 62mph
200kph = 124mph
300kph = 186mph
400kph = 249mph

What James took to the North Pole

To cheer himself up, James brought along a few special treats...

I **don't** like snow. I **hate** being cold. I **hate** outdoor pursuits. I **hate** the idea that I've got to push my body to find the limit. I **can't stand** this stupid clothing that makes this rustling noise when you move.

- A big bag of **chocolate**, including a 'Mr Big' bar for Jezza – a Canadian favourite made of vanilla wafer

topped with caramel, peanuts and rice crispies, covered in chocolate. And 300 calories, which is useful – apparently you need 5,000 calories a day when trekking across the Arctic. (Maybe not if you're driving, Jeremy.)

- A tin of **SPAM®**, to celebrate with once they got to the Pole. SPAM® is chopped pork and ham, and 983 calories per tin – useful energy when you're digging a Toyota out of a snowdrift. James ate it, even though Jeremy shot the tin to bits.

- **Quail's eggs**. Much smaller than chicken eggs, with speckled shells and a stronger taste. Jeremy was disappointed that James forgot the celery salt to have with them.

- **Paté de foie gras**. Made from goose or duck livers (foie gras is French for 'fatty liver'). The birds are fed lots of food to make their livers as big as possible.

- 24-month-old parmigiano **cheese** – a Stravecchio, in fact (meaning 'extra-aged'). Parmigiano (or parmesan) is a firm Italian cheese often grated over pasta.

- **Salmon eggs**. Reddish-orange balls like tiny redcurrants, they're soft, salty and fishy. They're also used as bait by fishermen. Sturgeon eggs are better known as caviar.

- Some warm **coffee**, which came in handy when Jeremy froze a metal nut to his lips.

- A **plastic bottle** with his name on, to wee in during the night.

Richard Attempts to Bury the Lacetti

When the Chevrolet Lacetti was retired as the Reasonably Priced Car, Richard was given the job of providing a suitably heroic send-off. Unfortunately.

Richard had all the right ingredients for a dramatic burial. Two 550-ft tall industrial chimneys, weighing 7185 tons each, ready to be demolished? Check. 25kg of nitroglycerine to blow them up? Check. Some fences and security guards to keep people from getting hurt? Check.

All he had to do was park the Lacetti next to the chimney, and wait for someone to press a big round red button. (It's always a big round red button, isn't it? Never a little purple switch. Funny, that.)

And, to give him his due, it certainly looked like he'd chosen the right spot – about three metres away, on the side the chimney was meant to fall down. But... when the BRRB was pressed... and the explosives went off... and the chimney fell over... the awkward truth was revealed. (Once the smoke had cleared, anyway.) He'd bodged it up. Made a hash of it. Muffed it. Blown it. Somehow the 170-metre tall chimney, three metres away from the car, had practically missed it.

Ah. You know, I can **just** see the nose of the car sticking out.

It was flattened, true. But definitely, and conclusively, not buried. Not good enough, Hammond. In a word: **useless**.

Nine Good Things about the Ford Fiesta

After a thorough road test, Top Gear declared the new Ford Fiesta to be a very good car indeed. Here are the reasons why.

THE NEW FORD FIESTA IS...

1 Practical. There is room in the boot for a zebra's head.

2 Economical. It is 40kg lighter than its predecessor, meaning better fuel economy. The most economical diesel engine is so clean that it doesn't even qualify for road tax.

3 Good to drive. It has a Volkswagen feel of solidity and a Lotus feel of sportiness, says Jeremy.

4 Fast. It will easily do 70mph. That's the maximum speed you can do in Britain.

5 Reliable. It won't break down, because it's made by Germans.

6 **Easy to park.** It has windows and a steering wheel. What more do you need?

7 **Able to outrun baddies in a Corvette through a shopping centre.** It has good grip, front-wheel-drive and a modest amount of power, which is exactly what you want when trying to escape baddies on a marble surface!

The baddy has made the classic baddy error. He's got **too much** power.

8 **Green.** Just look at it!

9 **Capable of taking part in a beach assault with the Royal Marines.** It fits on the Marine's LCVP MkV landing craft with room to spare, and smoke grenades fit perfectly in the cupholders. Look at this for a beach assault craft!

Are we there yet?

The World's Fastest Trains

The Japanese bullet train couldn't outrun Jeremy in a Nissan GT-R, but then again, it isn't the fastest train in the world...

Shanghai Maglev, China

Speed: 268mph
This amazing train doesn't run on rails at all, but is instead suspended above the track by a series of hugely powerful magnets. It has exactly the same top speed as the Bugatti Veyron Super Sport!

CRH, China

Speed: 220mph
The world's fastest train debuted this year in China. It can race between the cities of Beijing and Tianjin, seventy miles apart, in under half an hour!

TGV, France

Speed: 192mph
France's high speed train line first ran in 1981, and still holds the record for the fastest cross-country average journey, including stops.

Korean Train Express, South Korea

Speed: 219mph
The fastest train in South Korea is only slightly slower than the record-holding Chinese train, but is normally limited to 186mph for safety reasons.

Shinkansen, Japan

Speed: 180mph
The Japanese call the bullet train 'Shinkansen', meaning 'new line'. It is one of the most reliable services in the world, and almost never runs late!

AVE, Spain

Speed: 180mph
Spain's high-speed rail network connects most of the major cities in the country, but it isn't cheap: some journeys can cost more than a plane flight!

High Speed One, Britain

Speed: 140mph
Britain's fastest rail line runs between London and the Channel Tunnel, but it's a yawning 80mph slower than China's speed machines...

The World's Greatest Police Cars

On Top Gear in 2008, Richard conclusively proved that the best cheap police car is a Suzuki Vitari with a rubber mat on the front. But if your national police force has a bit more cash to burn, how about one of these?

Italy: Lamborghini Gallardo

In 2009, Italian police crashed their 550bhp Gallardo into a line of parked cars, writing it off. They won't be too worried – they've got another one in the garage!

UK: Lotus Exige

In 2007, Sussex police acquired this 150mph Exige to help teach young drivers about road safety. While making them very jealous at the same time...

Germany: Brabus CLS V12 S Rocket

Say hello to the most powerful police car in the world. Brabus tuned up this Mercedes CLS to 730bhp and donated it to the German police force. With a top speed of 225mph, any car chases will be very short-lived...

Austria: Porsche 911

Police cars usually have criminals in the back, but Austria's 911 has something more powerful wedged behind the policemen up front: the engine!

USA: Carbon Motors E7

This mean-looking diesel patrol car is described as 'the world's first purpose-built police car'. American cops are expecting to get their first spin in the E7 in 2012...

Lincolnshire, UK: Tractor

Yes, while Italian police get Lamborghinis and Austrian police get Porsches, the coppers in Lincolnshire are stuck with a John Deere tractor to spread the message of rural safety...

Cars that Are Better than they Look

VW Phaeton

It looks a bit safe and boring, but it's engineered to phenomenal standards; the air-conditioning will work all day in a desert at 100mph,

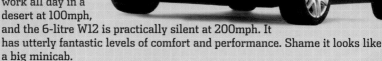

and the 6-litre W12 is practically silent at 200mph. It has utterly fantastic levels of comfort and performance. Shame it looks like a big minicab.

Porsche Cayenne Turbo

Jeremy thought it was brilliantly engineered, phenomenal off-road, superb on-road, powerful and comfortable. But the look of it... 'I have seen more attractive gangrenous wounds than this. It is a monkfish among cars. It has the sex appeal of a camel with gingivitis. And frankly I would rather walk back to the studio than drive another yard in it. So I shall.'

Porsche Panamera

A lovely Porsche, stretched to fit in four doors – which turns it into an absolutely horrible-looking monster. All the chaps loved driving it, but hated looking at it.

Porsche Boxster Spyder

Are you seeing a theme here? Jeremy mocked the cloth roof that looked like a tramp's hat, and that it had no door handles, air con, or radio and still costs £44,000. However it only weighs 1250kg, can do 166mph, and only needs 4.8s to get from 0-60 thanks to a clever gearbox called Doppelkupplungsgetriebe (gotta love the Germans).

BMW M3 CSL

It's the shape of a four-door saloon driven by salesmen with Bluetooth earpieces, but it isn't one. It has a carbon fibre roof, a plastic boot (with a cardboard floor), no electric thingummys, or air con, or radio. All of which weight-saving makes it as light as a butterfly; add racing tyres and a 355bhp, 3.2 litre engine... As Jeremy says, 'It's BMW at its absolute best.'

Any rental car

You may think your parents are the most boring drivers on the planet. But get them on holiday in a rental car... suddenly they discover hidden magical powers and start driving like they actually enjoy it. All rental cars, whatever they look like, have this amazing ability to transform dull school-run drivers into F1 challengers.

Cars that Look Better than they Are

Nissan 350Z

Designed by an Indian from Leicester, and built by the Japanese for the Americans. 'It's a raw hamburger curry served in a disinterested way on a garlicky jus,' according to Jeremy. It's got a loud stereo, a rubbish noisy French engine, it's exhausting to drive and the ride is uncomfortably hard. The build quality is flimsy, and there are no back seats or boot space. 'C-, 3 out of 10. Could do better.'

MG X-Power SV

With its carbon fibre body, it's pretty exciting to look at, and has a stupendous engine noise; but it's all a bit of a mess inside. No satnav, no electric seats, no airbag, heavy gears, an ugly dash with dodgy dials, no space for Jeremy's left leg... and it gobbles a kilo of fuel every minute at top speed. Oh, and it's £75,000 for the base model. You could get a much better car for that.

Jeremy's Ford GT

His dream car, right up until he actually got it home. Too wide for British roads, gulps petrol, tiny tank so he had to refuel constantly, no rear view so it was impossible to reverse, no boot space, the doors overlap the roof so you need an acre of space to get in and out. Ford thought it was being stolen – while he was still in it. 'The thing is, I think I'm right in saying that I have never completed a single journey, anywhere there and back, in it **ever**. Which must make it the most unreliable car... ever made.'

RX56 TZD

Honda Civic Type R (3rd generation)

Much snazzier to look at than the previous version, but bigger and heavier, with no more power. This makes it slower. Jeremy also didn't like the cheaper suspension, the understeer, the spoiler that blocks the back window, the beeping ignition, the seat adjustment and the ride comfort. 'This is completely unacceptable. You need a skeleton made of granite. I like hot hatchbacks, I always have done, but this one is hopeless.'

Chevrolet Corvette ZR1

It looks like a really exciting toy. But Jeremy said it was plasticky and flimsy, started to fall apart while he was testing it and was insane to drive, like riding a lion made of teeth and jelly. 'All wobbly, and then it bites your arm off.' Anyone who isn't the Stig that tried to drive it fast would definitely die.

TVR Tuscan 2

Very quick and looks excellent. But no traction control or anti-lock brakes, so it skids like a dog wearing socks on a polished floor. The windscreen wiper doesn't work above 80mph. The door handles are on the underneath of the wing mirrors, and the ignition is... hidden somewhere insane. Richard thought it was too difficult and complicated and smelled like a canoe factory because of all the plastic and fibreglass.

Chrysler Crossfire

Some people adore the looks of this thing, but Jeremy didn't. 'It looks like a dog doing a poo; it's slow, uncomfortable, expensive, and cursed with a cramped, badly trimmed interior, an awful gearbox and no back seats. The engine doesn't make a particularly sporty noise, the ride is terrible, and it isn't especially economical.'

Road Signs You Don't Need to Know

Diversion ENDS – because surely I'm back on the road I wanted to be on in the first place?

Falling rocks – unless you've got a corrugated tin roof like James in Iceland, what exactly can you do about it?

Cows, sheep, frogs, ducks, hedgehogs – the trouble with all of these is that animals *can't read signs*. So they don't appear in the places they're meant to. Either that, or you're driving in a field.

Tractors – you can meet tractors absolutely everywhere in the countryside. So this should appear every hundred metres. You may as well have a sign saying 'grass'.

No vehicles carrying explosives – What? Exploding cars? Who the flip has explosives in their car?

No entry 'except for access' – well of course I want access. Why on earth would I be trying to drive down here otherwise?

Except for access

Keep in low gear – to be honest, I think I can make that sort of decision myself... since I'm the one doing the driving

Keep in low gear

HEAVY PLANT CROSSING

Heavy Plant Crossing – doesn't that mean there's a giant vegetable competition ahead?

Cattle grid – unless you're riding a micro scooter, you should be able to get over one of these. So why do we need to be told about it?

Cattle grid

Aircraft – how tall do you think my car is anyway? Only Jeremy's campervan could be a threat to low-flying planes.

Level crossing without gate – it's useful to know there's a rail crossing ahead, but is it *really* only used by steam engines?

Ascari A10 vs Daihatsu Materia

In 2007, Jeremy sensibly reviewed the Ascari A10 against one of its closest rivals, the, errr, Daihatsu Materia. He decided that, on balance, he preferred the Ascari. But how do the two match up on paper?

	Ascari A10	Daihatsu Materia
Price	£350,000	**£11,000**
Engine	**5.0-litre V8**	1.4-litre four-cylinder
Power	**625bhp**	102bhp
0-60mph	**2.8 secs**	10.8 secs
Cornering	**Berzerk!**	Sensible
Noise	**Deafening!**	Nice and quiet
Looks	**Amazing**	Boring
Fuel economy	Not great	**Pretty impressive**
Seats	Two	**Five**
Boot	Tiny	**Nice and big**
Airbag	Definitely not	**Yes**
Result	6 points	5 points

It's a close thing, but *Top Gear* Science proves that the Ascari A10 is the better car. But only just...

This car is **insanely** fast!

The World's Greatest Endurance Races

In 2007, the boys entered the Britcar 24-hour race in their diesel BMW. But that epic endurance battle is a walk in the park compared to this lot...

The 24 Hours of Le Mans

The daddy of them all. The 24 Hours of Le Mans has been held annually since 1923, and has been won by some of the greatest drivers in history. Run on the 8.2-mile 'Circuit de la Sarthe', the race was won in 2010 by Audi's diesel-powered R15, which covered a record-breaking 3246 miles in the 24-hour period!

The 12 Hours of Sebring

Though only half as long as Le Mans, the 12-hour Sebring race is just as demanding on drivers. Held in the hot, sticky Florida swamps, the 12 Hours of Sebring – first held in 1950 – has destroyed many of the world's greatest sports cars.

Hey get out, it's my turn!

The 24 Hours of Daytona

Along with Le Mans and Sebring, Daytona makes up the 'Triple Crown' of endurance racing. Only ten drivers in history have won all three races – and two of them are English: Jackie Oliver and Andy Wallace.

Nürburgring 24 Hours

The Nurburgring 'Nordschliefe' – the giant, windy forest circuit that made Sabine Schmitz into a legend – is one of the scariest racetracks in the world. Imagine racing it at full speed, in the middle of the night, having not slept for two days. Scary, huh?

The Rules of 24-Hour Racing

Competing in an endurance race isn't simply a case of turning up at a race track and driving until you fall asleep. Twenty-four-hour racing has a set of rules and regulations all of its own...

At least three drivers

In the early days of endurance racing, there were no limits on the minimum number of drivers for a single car. This meant that some drivers tried to drive for the entire twenty-four hours – a very dangerous plan! Since the 1990s, rules have dictated that each team must have at least three drivers. It helps if one of these drivers is the Stig.

Top Gear took four drivers to the BritCar 24-hour race

No more than fourteen hours

Of course, even if you have three drivers in your team, two of them could do nothing more than a half-minute stint, leaving one driver to race for twenty-three hours. To stop this happening, the rules state that no driver can drive for more than a total of fourteen hours.

The Stig did more than his fair share of driving – luckily!

They struggled to make the start — but they did finish . . . just

Classy cars

Unlike Formula One, in which all the cars on the grid adhere to the same rules, endurance races will usually feature cars from a number of different 'classes'. As well as racing for overall victory, cars will also compete to win their class. So, even, if a team finishes fiftieth overall, they can still claim victory for being the fastest car of their type in the race.

Top Gear finished 3rd in their class. Not bad, chaps

Crossing the finish line

In order to finish the race, a car must cross the start-finish line after the twenty-four hour clock has counted down to zero. So if you crash out on the last corner, even if you've completed twenty laps more than your nearest rival, you won't win the race!

How to go to the Toilet in a Car

If you drive from Bordeaux towards Spain, the gutter is littered with big water bottles... full of truck drivers' wee.* Nice. Isn't there a more civilized way to relieve yourself in a car?

Wee in a bottle

Jeremy tried to drive from London to Edinburgh and back on one tank of fuel. He was determined not to stop for anything...

Jeremy: 'Six hours on the road. I think I need a wee, but I can't stop because that would mean starting the engine again, and starting the engine uses a load of fuel. So... New York taxi driver trick. And you're not allowed to watch.'

Wee in a bag

Richard and James spent twenty-four hours in a Smart car, which meant there came a point when nature called...

Richard: 'Mate, I'm gonna have to go. I'm sorry. It's not so bad though, because I bought... these! Weebags. It's for... you have a pee in it.'

James: 'Oh my God, that's hideous!'

Richard: 'You wee in that end and its got special crystals that turn into a gel and they absorb your pee.'

Wee on the floor

If you're in the middle of nowhere, then fit a bumper dumper; a loo seat that fixes on to the tow hitch. Just remember who's using it.

Clarkson! I know it's you, you insufferable oaf! **I'm on the throne!**

* Known in the trade as 'lorry pop'.

Wee on the seat

In the middle of their twenty-four-hour race, the tame racing driver came over all human...

> Having a pee right now... aah. A little present for Jeremy.

And later, so did Richard.

Richard: 'Right now, the computers tell us that the Stig is having a wee in the car. And I'm next.'

Professional racing drivers are usually better at holding it than this. They go before a race and manage to hold it – and they sweat so much, it's not usually an issue. Though there's plenty of rumours about famous drivers wetting themselves...

Wee in a box

You can buy a folded cardboard box that opens out into a perfectly useable toilet. However it needs to be set up properly, and Jeremy isn't very good at following instructions. He ended up flat on his back, surrounded by people laughing at him.

> Bear in mind you have to erect this while **desperate** for a number two, with lorries going by.

Let's face it, there's simply no acceptable alternative to:
a) going before you set off,
b) waiting until you get there, or
c) stopping at a proper loo on the way.
   And don't forget to wash your hands.

107

Supercar Locator Map

And which country makes the most, eh?

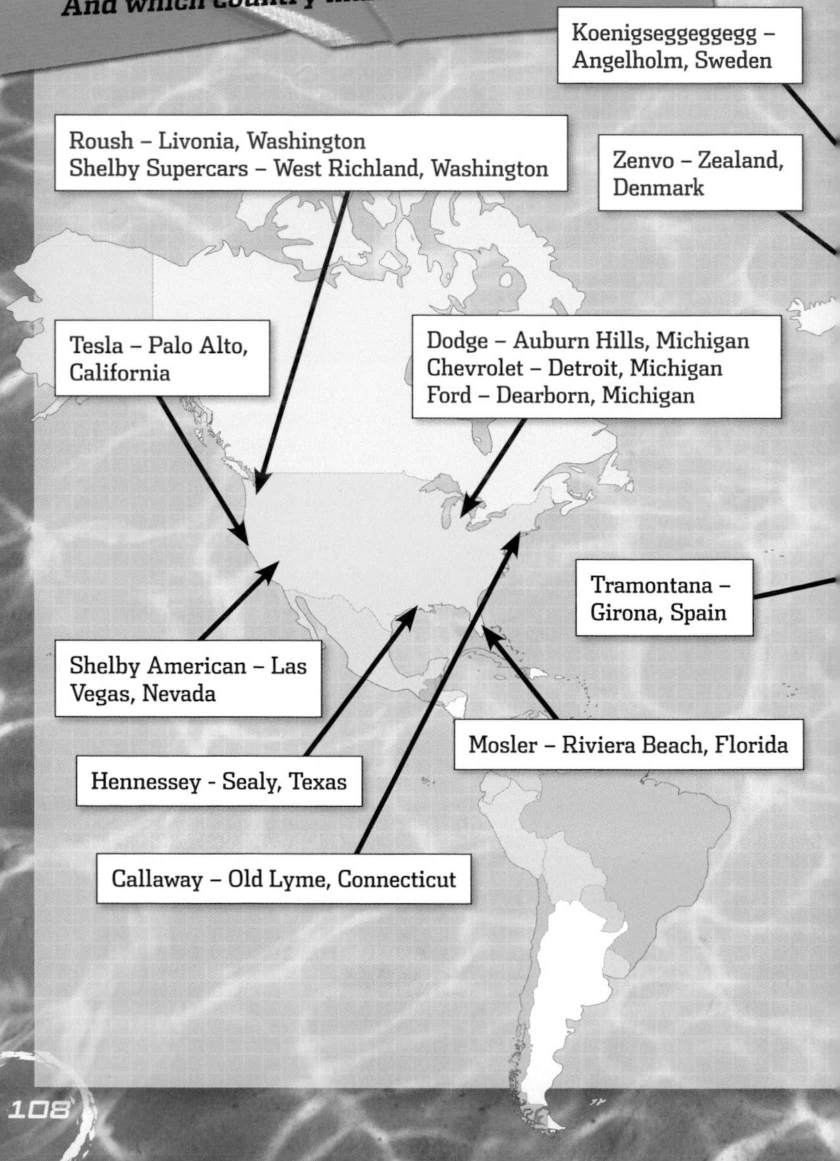

Koenigseggeggegg – Angelholm, Sweden

Roush – Livonia, Washington
Shelby Supercars – West Richland, Washington

Zenvo – Zealand, Denmark

Tesla – Palo Alto, California

Dodge – Auburn Hills, Michigan
Chevrolet – Detroit, Michigan
Ford – Dearborn, Michigan

Tramontana – Girona, Spain

Shelby American – Las Vegas, Nevada

Mosler – Riviera Beach, Florida

Hennessey - Sealy, Texas

Callaway – Old Lyme, Connecticut

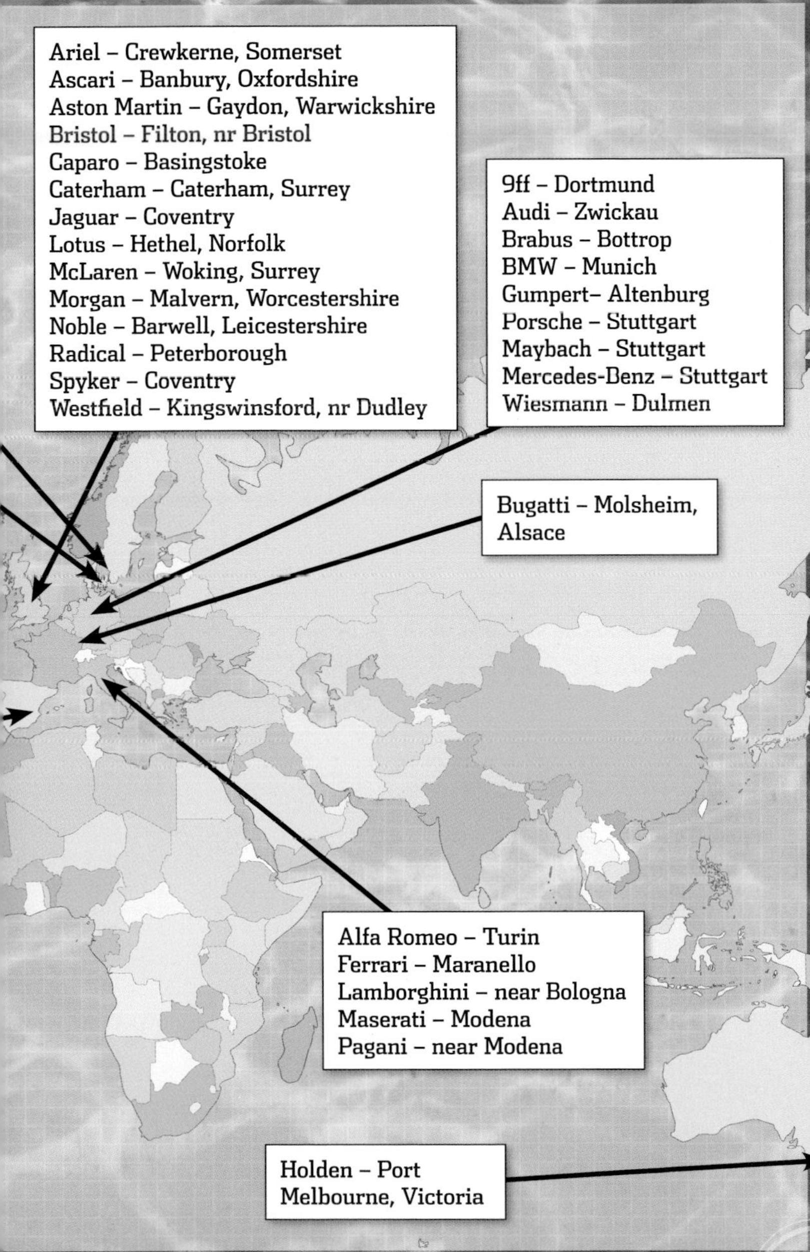

Ariel – Crewkerne, Somerset
Ascari – Banbury, Oxfordshire
Aston Martin – Gaydon, Warwickshire
Bristol – Filton, nr Bristol
Caparo – Basingstoke
Caterham – Caterham, Surrey
Jaguar – Coventry
Lotus – Hethel, Norfolk
McLaren – Woking, Surrey
Morgan – Malvern, Worcestershire
Noble – Barwell, Leicestershire
Radical – Peterborough
Spyker – Coventry
Westfield – Kingswinsford, nr Dudley

9ff – Dortmund
Audi – Zwickau
Brabus – Bottrop
BMW – Munich
Gumpert– Altenburg
Porsche – Stuttgart
Maybach – Stuttgart
Mercedes-Benz – Stuttgart
Wiesmann – Dulmen

Bugatti – Molsheim, Alsace

Alfa Romeo – Turin
Ferrari – Maranello
Lamborghini – near Bologna
Maserati – Modena
Pagani – near Modena

Holden – Port Melbourne, Victoria

Family Tree of Car Makers

Blimey, this is complicated. It turns out everyone owns everyone else, for a start. And this doesn't even include the dozens of Chinese firms making millions of cars you've never heard of. And it'll all be different in about half an hour.

Ram

Chrysler

Chrysler Group, LLC

Dodge

Jeep

Tata

Jaguar

Tata Motors, Ltd

Land Rover

Proton Holdings, Bhd

Proton

Daewoo

Lotus

A lot of unknown Chinese brands

Volvo

Geely Automobile

50%

London black cabs

Ferrari

Maserati

85%

Lancia

Fiat

Fiat

Abarth

Alfa Romeo

Rolls-Royce

BMW

BMW AG

Mini

Ford

Ford Motor Company

Holden

Lincoln

Chevrolet

Buick

General Motors Company

GMC

Opel (Vauxhall)

Cadillac

Toyota Motor Corporation

Lexus

Scion

51%

Daihatsu

Toyota

110

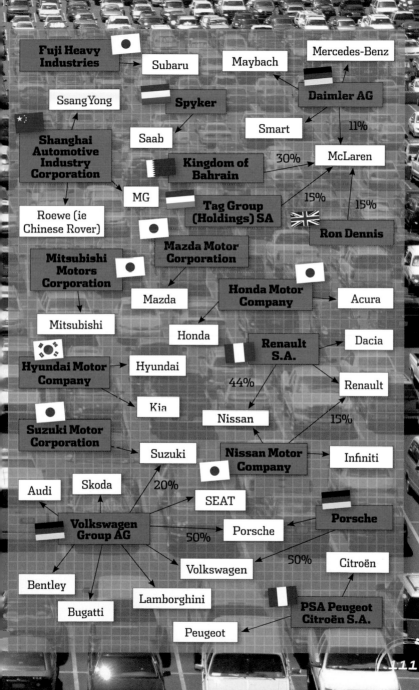

National Racing Colours

Ever wondered why Lotuses are often green, Ferraris tend to be red and Porsches prefer silver?

It's all to do with the traditional national racing colours. In the early twentieth century, early international motor racing rules required cars to be painted by country, and somehow these colours stuck...

Britain: Green

Because many of the earliest British motor races were actually held in Ireland, UK cars adopted the Irish national colour. British Racing Green was famously used by Bentley before the Second World War, and by the F1 cars of Lotus and Cooper in the 1950s and 1960s.

Italy: Red

Ferrari – Italy's most famous manufacturer – is the company most closely linked to the 'Rosso Corsa' paint job, but it was the super-successful Alfa Romeo race cars of the 1920s that made sure Italy would forever be associated with red cars.

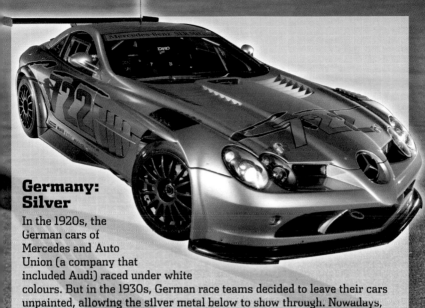

Germany: Silver

In the 1920s, the German cars of Mercedes and Auto Union (a company that included Audi) raced under white colours. But in the 1930s, German race teams decided to leave their cars unpainted, allowing the silver metal below to show through. Nowadays, Porsche, Audi and Mercedes racers often wear silver.

France: Blue

The French have used blue – or *bleu*, as they call it – as their national colour since the twelfth century. The beautiful Bugattis of the 1920s brought bright blue French race cars to fame, but they weren't as fast as the modern Veyron! This version celebrates 100 years of Bugatti.

And a few more:

USA: Blue and white stripes. **Japan:** White with a red dot.
Finland: White with blue stripes

113

Why do Petrolheads Love the Isle of Man?

Back in 2005, the boys headed to the Isle of Man to test out the Aston Martin V8 Vantage, BMW M6 and Porsche 911. But why is the little island such a special place for petrolheads?

The Isle of Man lies between England, North Wales, Scotland and Northern Ireland in the Irish Sea. It is thirty-two miles long and just fourteen miles wide. About 80,000 people live on the island.

The first motor races were held on the Isle of Man in the early twentieth century. In 1903, the British government imposed a speed limit of 20mph on UK roads, making road races impossible – but this law did not apply to the Isle of Man.

The Isle of Man's first road race took place in 1904, on a fifty-two-mile stretch of public road called the 'Highlands Course'. It was won by a gentleman called Clifford Earl, who completed five laps of the circuit in seven and a half hours at an average speed of 34mph!

In the following years, dozens of car races were held on the Isle of Man, but the island's mountain roads

for motorcycle races. In the 1930s, the Isle of Man TT – a high speed motorbike race around the island – became the most **famous** bike race in the world.

Today, the Isle of Man TT is one of the most **popular** bike races in the world. Held in May and June each year, thousands of bikers head to the island to set their best time on the thirty-eight-mile street circuit. The fastest man ever to lap the course is fifteen-time winner John McGuinness in 2007, who completed his fastest lap at an average speed of 130mph!

High speed plus hedges, trees, buildings and telegraph poles makes the Isle of Man TT one of the most **dangerous** races in the world. Between 1907 and 2009, 231 riders were killed on the course.

Even today, there are no speed limits on the Isle of Man. However, there are speed restrictions in urban areas, and the police will quickly arrest anyone driving recklessly on the mountain roads!

Stig in an X-Bow

Electric Dreams

Hybrids like the Toyota Prius and Honda Insight – cars that run on a combination of electric power and petrol or diesel – are ten-a-penny at the moment. But what about all-electric cars?

Tesla Roadster

This sleek sports car is based on the Lotus Elise but, as Jeremy discovered in 2008, it'll outrun the petrol-powered car from Norfolk, hitting 60mph in under four seconds!

Tango

It might look like it's about to topple over, but the tall, narrow Tango is astonishingly fast. It'll hit 60mph in around four seconds and won't stop accelerating until it hits 150mph!

G-Wiz

Oh dear. There are some brilliant electric cars out there... and then there's the G-Wiz. Technically, it's not even a car. Its maker, Indian company Riva, says it's a 'heavy quadricycle'.

Hammerhead i-Thrust

Challenged to build a better electric car than the G-Wiz, the boys came up with this boxy monstrosity. It was slow, dangerous and constantly running out of battery... but at least it had a great name.

Mini E

Minis usually run on petrol or diesel, but, since 2009, this all-electric version has been available in the USA. Just one tiny problem: you can't actually buy it, but only lease it from Mini for a few months!

Peugeot EX1

You'll never be allowed to drive it on the road, but the EX1 racer has set a bunch of electric car world records in the track. From a standing start, it'll cover a mile in just forty-one seconds!

Nissan Leaf

Expected to hit the road in 2011, the Leaf will be the first of dozens of all-electric family cars from the world's biggest manufacturers. Nissan says it can manage 140 miles between charging – provided you drive carefully!

Knight XV

A firm in Canada confidently thinks there are one hundred people in the world who want one of these: the Knight XV. We'll see, shall we?

The Specs

- **Price:** starts from $489,000
- **Weight:** 5.896 tons – that's the same as two Porsche Cayennes and a Ford Focus glued together!
- **Height:** 2.5m
- **Length:** 6.1m
- **Width:** 2.5m
- **Engine:** 6.0l V8, 325hp (which gives a power to weight ratio of only 55hp/ton – the same as a 1993 Ford Fiesta)
- **Fuel tank:** 238 litres, and it probably needs all of that to get to the shops
- Two air con units (one in the front, another in the back)
- Night-vision cameras front & rear
- Huge 20-inch aluminium wheels with forty-inch tyres that still work if they're shot
- Wilton wool carpets

- Ultrasuede leather interior
- Two TVs in the rear with remote control
- Laptop rests
- Protective firewall between the engine and passenger compartment
- That's not glass in the windows, it's 6cm-thick 'transparent armour'. The rest is made of high strength steel, ballistic aluminium and other very strong things. Before making the Knight XV, they fire bullets at it – this monster is bulletproof for up to twenty-four hours!

It doesn't end there. You can add an external listening system, an under-vehicle magnetic attachment detector, searchlights, a GPS transmitter, an oxygen survival kit and external smoke security system – it's the Batmobile!

How do Radio-Controlled Cars Work?

No, it's not magic. It's science, which is another thing entirely.

1 You hold a controller, which contains a radio transmitter, powered by batteries. Simple versions have one stick for going forwards or backwards, and one for steering left or right. Fancier versions may have a wheel for

steering, a trigger for speed and even buttons for gears and headlights. The controller sends out a radio signal all the time, which varies as you move the controls.

2 The car contains a receiver, again powered by batteries. This picks up the radio signal and translates it into specific signals for the different parts of the car. Each part of the car (engine, steering, lights and so on) is controlled by a different signal or channel.

3 The steering channel goes to a servo, a lever like a tiny mechanical muscle: depending on the signal it gets, it will turn one way or the other. This servo is connected to the front wheels (or in a full-size car, to the steering wheel).

4 The engine channel goes to a speed controller, which adjusts the amount of power going to the main motor or engine.

5 The motor may be electric, powered by batteries, or internal combustion (like a full-size car), powered by a special mix of nitromethane, methanol and oil. Better cars have lighter, more powerful motors and need expensive batteries.

6 Off-road cars have bigger tyres and better suspension; road cars, er, don't.

7 You can get reasonably priced 'toy' RC cars, which you can't really modify; or bigger, more expensive 'hobby' cars, with better components that you can upgrade or adjust, that go much faster. Or you could go the whole hog, and fit the kit in a real car, and crash it into a caravan!

Greatest Film and TV Cars

James Bond has had some pretty good cars, but he doesn't look after them. His lovely Aston Martin DBS V12 was rolled 7.5 times (a world record) in *Casino Royale*, which did it no good at all. Here are some of his other better cars.

- **Aston Martin V12 Vanquish** with cloaking device, missiles, machine guns, ejector seat and ice-spikes (*Die Another Day*)
- **BMW 750iL** which can be remotely driven by phone, is bullet & hammer proof, has a cable-cutter, tear-gas, rockets, caltrops and self-inflating tyres (*Tomorrow Never Dies*)
- **Aston Martin V8 Vantage Volante** has ice-spikes, skis, missiles, laser and rocket booster and can self-destruct *(The Living Daylights)*
- **Lotus Esprit** squirts oil, turns into a submarine with missiles, depth charges and torpedoes, and can self-destruct (*The Spy Who Loved Me*)
- **Aston Martin DB5** with machine guns, ejector seat, bulletproof shield, rotating number plates, oil and water jets, smoke screen, tracking radar and tyre-slashing blades (*Goldfinger*)

Other excellent film and TV cars:

- The **Batmobile** has changed over the years and has always been so full of gadgets it's amazing it can move. Various versions have had cable-cutters, parachutes, lasers, grappling hooks, machine guns, rockets, jet engines, tracking radar, computers, ejector seat, fire extinguishers, video phone, bomb-proof shields, nail/oil/smoke/bomb dispensers and can self-destruct after turning two wheels into a motorbike. Phew!

- **Bumblebee** from *Transformers* may look like a Chevrolet Camaro, but he's actually an alien robot. And is available from a toyshop near you.

- **FAB 1** from *Thunderbirds* is pink (unfortunately), has six wheels and was enormous; but it could fly, had skis, bulletproof tyres and an escape pod.
- **Chitty Chitty Bang Bang** is a vintage racing car (from the film of the same name) with lots of leather, polished wood and brass... and secret wings, propellers and inflatable floats. (Ian Fleming wrote the original book, as well as the James Bond stories.)
- The *Back to the Future* films revolve around a **DeLorean DMC-12** fitted with a time machine. It has to be moving at 88mph to activate, but watch out for the nuclear reactor in the back. In the future, it also gets a hover-conversion so it can fly.
- **Herbie** is an unassuming VW Beetle (from several films) with a lot of personality. He goes faster than you'd think. But he's still a Beetle.
- **KITT** from *Knight Rider* is a Ford Shelby GT500KR, controlled by a very clever computer. It can talk, change to look like other cars, perform massive jet-assisted jumps, change your fingerprints, print small 3-D objects and has lasers, machine guns, missiles, projector screens, first aid kit and dispensers for slippery black ice, anti-missile flares and tear gas.
- The **General Lee** is a Dodge Charger driven by Bo and Luke Duke, *The Dukes of Hazzard*. The doors are welded shut (for safety, apparently, but mainly because it looks cool). In an old TV series and a recent film, the General Lee does loads of jumps, drifting and racing. Your dad loved this car.

Planes of the RAF

In 2007, Richard raced the Bugatti Veyron against the Royal Air Force's Typhoon Eurofighter. He lost. But how does the amazing Eurofighter compare to the RAF's other planes?

Eurofighter Typhoon F2

Year introduced: 2003
Power: 40,000lb of thrust
Maximum speed: 1320mph
Maximum altitude: 65,000 feet
Number of crew: 1

Tornado F3

Year introduced: 1985
Power: 33,000lb of thrust
Maximum speed: 1450mph
Maximum altitude: 50,000 feet
Number of crew: 2

Tornado GR4

Year introduced: 2003
Power: 32,000lb of thrust
Maximum speed: 858mph
Maximum altitude: 50,000 feet
Number of crew: 2

Harrier GR9

Year introduced: 2006
(now decommissioned)
Power: 40,000lb of thrust
Maximum speed: 660mph
Maximum altitude:
43,000 feet
Number of crew: 1

Nimrod R1

Year introduced: 1969
Power: 48,000lb of thrust
Maximum speed: 415mph
Maximum altitude:
44,000 feet
Number of crew: 29

Sentry AEW1

Power: 96,000lb of thrust
Maximum speed: 528mph
Maximum altitude: 35,000 feet
Number of crew: 18

How to Play a Vuvuzela

Every spectator at the 2010 World Cup seemed to be playing a vuvuzela, but Jeremy and James couldn't get a note out of the plastic horn. Here's how to make music on South Africa's favourite instrument...

One: Acquire a vuvuzela. This is very important.

Two: Purse your lips and use your cheek muscles to push your lips forward.

Three:

Put the narrow end of the vuvuzela firmly against your mouth. Don't put your lips around it!

Four: Blow hard into the vuvuzela, vibrating your lips against the mouthpiece. The vuvuzela should make a noise like a elephant trumpeting loudly.

Five: Loosen or tighten your lips to create different notes. With a bit of practise, you'll be belting out the *Top Gear* theme tune!

They don't work!

127

The Six Worst Special Edition Cars Ever!

It seems some manufacturers just can't help producing hideous 'special editions'. Sometimes they're to honour a celebrity, sometimes they're just because there were a few tins of pink paint lying around the factory going to waste. Whatever the reason, get rid of them!

Volkswagen Polo Harlequin

No, this Polo wasn't stuck together by a colour-blind VW employee. Every single Harlequin Polo looked as confused as this one.

Fiat Seicento Schumacher

In 2001, Michael Schumacher won his fourth world title, defeating David Coulthard by a massive fifty-eight points. In honour of this achievement, Fiat released a bright yellow city car with just 58bhp. Oh dear.

Fiat 500 Barbie

Barbie turned fifty in 2009. She looks good for her age. To commemorate the event, a bright pink Fiat 500 was released. People felt very ill.

Land Rover Lara Croft

What would the Tomb Raider star drive if she was real and, er, not a collection of pixels? Probably not this lumpy Land Rover...

Ferrari 599 China

The 599 GTB is an amazing car, one of the very best in the world. Unless it's covered in a greeny wrap that makes its surface look like cracked porcelain. Yuck.

Citroen C4 Loeb

Sebastien Loeb is the greatest rally driver of all time, with seven world championships to his name. Surely he deserves better than a C4 hatchback with exactly no more power or special rally bits?

Races You Can Go and See

You've seen them on the show, but where can you actually see some of those lovely cars? At a racetrack, of course.

Kart racing – Schumacher and Fernando Alonso started in karts when they were children.

Autotesting – what Jeremy did against the Germans in a Mini. A short series of manoeuvres, on tarmac, marked by cones, with time penalties for hitting cones or going the wrong way. Develops high-speed precision skills of the kind you see in display shows.

Autocross – temporary races set up by amateur clubs on grass or stubble fields, racing road cars. Very cheap to compete in. Cars usually race in pairs and are timed.

Autograss – again, a temporary track on grass or stubble, but a simple short oval track with all cars racing together. TG did this in their non-Porsche coupes... for four hours.

BTCC The BTCC specification allows a wide variety of cars that still look pretty much like road cars rather than racing cars, including VWs, BMWs, Fords and Hondas. It's cheap and simple enough for independent private teams to enter alongside works teams. The racing is exciting with plenty of overtaking and 'contact' (= 'crashes'). Races can be short and furious or long endurance tests. The drivers are good enough to race buses and motorhomes with Richard Hammond.

Demolition derby – using knackered cars, that are deliberately destroyed. The last car moving wins. Can be run on a figure-of-eight track, to guarantee crashes.

Drag races – short, straight timed races, usually held over 1/4 mile or

1/8 mile. Cars can race in pairs. Top fuel dragsters can reach 329mph in 4.5s, subjecting the drivers to a face-altering 3.4g (see page 155)

F1 – the pinnacle of motor racing, according to its fans, with prices to match.

Folkrace – what James did in Finland. Anyone can ask to buy your car after the race, at a fixed price of about £600 and you have to sell it if you want to keep racing. So no one bothers to spend much on the cars – they're all practically wrecked already. Shortish tracks on gravel or tarmac, with the potential for nudging.

Hill-climbing – drivers race up a hill on a closed tarmac road, against the clock. In Britain the courses are short, covered in less than a minute. As James proved, small simple old cars can beat heavier, more complicated, new ones.

Rallying – special stage rallying is on closed public roads or off-road areas. Cars have to cover several sections a day, with limited access to spares and repairs. The driver doesn't always know where he's going; the co-pilot reads him notes to warn what's ahead. Road rallies and regularity rallies use public roads, normal or vintage cars and stick to the speed limit.

Rallycross – a cross between rallying and touring car racing, on tracks combining tarmac and gravel. Fast and furious, with short races – up to sixty in a day. You can start competing in rallycross when you're fourteen. Cars include Citroen Saxos, Suzuki Swifts and Peugeot 205 GTis.

Sports car racing – what all those two-seater Porsches, Astons and Jags that *Top Gear* loves are for. As raced at Le Mans. In Britain, look for the British GT championships if you want to see an Ascari race a KTM X-Bow and an Aston Martin DBRS9.

Stock car racing – on short oval shale or tarmac courses, like where Richard went motorhome racing. Various classes, from custom built stock cars with huge angled wings on the roof, to strengthened road cars, to old bangers. Contact is allowed.

Track days – most racetracks run events when you can pay to bring your car and race against everyone else. There are hundreds of these every year. And don't forget that someone, somewhere, is racing *anything* with wheels. Trucks, shopping trolleys, lawn mowers, milk floats...

All the Countries that Drive on the Left (and Fourteen that Swapped)

- Anguilla
- Antigua
- Australia
- Bahamas
- Bangladesh
- Barbados
- Barbuda
- Bermuda
- Bhutan
- Botswana
- Brunei
- Cayman Islands
- Cyprus
- Dominica
- East Timor
- Falkland Islands
- Fiji
- Grenada
- Guyana
- Hong Kong
- India
- Indonesia
- Ireland
- Jamaica
- Japan
- Kenya
- Kiribati
- Lesotho
- Macau
- Malawi
- Malaysia
- Maldives
- Malta
- Mauritius
- Montserrat
- Mozambique
- Namibia
- Nauru
- Nepal
- New Zealand
- Niue
- Pakistan
- Papua New Guinea
- Saint Helena
- Saint Kitts and Nevis
- Saint Lucia
- Saint Vincent and the Grenadines
- Samoa
- Seychelles
- Solomon Islands
- South Africa
- Sri Lanka
- Suriname
- Swaziland
- Tanzania
- Thailand
- Tonga
- Trinidad and Tobago
- Turks and Caicos Islands
- United Kingdom
- Virgin Islands
- Zambia
- Zimbabwe

Did drive on the left, but switched to the right:

- Denmark (1793)
- Russia (1900s)
- Portugal (1920s)
- parts of Canada (1923)
- Czechoslovakia, Yugoslavia, Hungary and parts of Austria (1938-9)
- Panama (1943)
- Argentina and the Philippines (1945)
- China (1946)
- Sweden (5am on Sunday 3 September 1967)
- Iceland (6am on Sunday 26 May 1968)

How Sweden did it

Sweden took four years to prepare for H-day (from Högertrafik, 'right-hand traffic'). They held a song contest about the switch and put the logo on souvenirs (including underwear).

Junctions were fitted with extra signs on the other side of the road, which were covered in black plastic. New road markings were also painted, then taped over. Everyone also had to convert their headlamps (see What you have to do to drive your car abroad, p134). Non-essential traffic was banned from 1am, when workers began stripping off all the black plastic.

Any traffic on the road at 4.50am had to stop, swap over to the right and carry on at 5am. In Stockholm, it was too tricky to convert the trams, so they were scrapped and replaced with new buses. (Their old right-hand-drive buses were exported to Pakistan and Kenya.)

What You Have to Do to Drive Your Car Abroad

- First, and most importantly, **drive more carefully**. British drivers have fewer accidents than almost everyone else – but only while we're in Britain.
- If your number plate doesn't say GB, you need a **GB sticker** on the back of the car. You can also get magnetic GB plates, which sound like a good idea – but check there actually is some metal on the rear of your car. It may all be plastic or carbon fibre back there, in which case the magnet won't stick.
- In Britain your headlights shine higher on the left-hand side (to shine on signs and pedestrians). However, where they drive on the wrong side (see page 132) this means your headlights would shine in drivers' faces. So you need to stick **converters** on your headlights. These are either black (to block out some of the light) or clever plastic (to bend some light down). The converters have to be stuck in exactly the right place for your particular car, which will probably make your dad swear.
- In most of Abroad, you have to carry a red **warning triangle** that you have to set up fifty or 100 metres behind your car if you break down. They can be fiddly to set up, particularly in the dark, on a busy road, when you're a bit stressed – which is pretty much the only time you need them.

- In Austria, Belgium, Croatia, France, Italy and Spain you have to put on an attractive **high-visibility jacket** before you get out of your car (if you break down, not all the time). This means it has to be stuffed somewhere in the car, not at the bottom of the boot under all the luggage.
- You don't *have* to have a **first aid kit** in most of Abroad (except Austria and Croatia) but it's probably not a bad idea. Accidents can happen anywhere (as Jeremy, Richard and James have proved).
- If you get pulled over by the rozzers while you're Abroad, and they find something wrong with your car or your driving, they can issue an on-the-spot fine, which you have to pay straight away. So carry some **money**, even on the last day of your holiday when you're late for the ferry. Actually, especially then.
- In countries that get proper winters, you have to have proper **winter tyres** that are good enough to drive on snow. And in the gloomy north (Denmark, Sweden, Finland and Norway) you have to have your **headlights on** all the time.
- In Austria and Switzerland, you have to buy a **sticker** at the border that allows you to drive on the motorways.
- Not only are **radar detectors** illegal in Abroad, but if your satnav can tell you where speed cameras are, that's illegal too. You have to turn that feature off, or face a fine.
- If all this sounds a bit fiddly, bear in mind that it used to be much worse. Before about 1993, your headlights had to be **yellow** to drive in France. This meant Dad trying to paint the headlights with special paint while waiting to go on the ferry, and spilling it on his holiday trousers.

Things Jeremy has Powered with a V8 Engine

Jeremy firmly believes that everything in the world can be made better with the addition of a huge V8 engine. Here are his two most ridiculous overpowered creations.

V8 blender

The problem: Conventional food blenders are boring, underpowered and take far too long to mulch ingredients into a tasty smoothie. Especially if those ingredients include, say, raw beef and a brick (see page 32).

The solution: Connect a V8 engine to it!

Does it work? No. V8 blender is so powerful that it simply blows the lid off the mixing bowl, spraying your kitchen/television studio with meat and brick.

Conclusion: Larger, sturdier mixing bowl needed.

Nice earmuffs, Jeremy

James tests the smoothie

V8 rocking chair

The problem: Old people struggle to reach the television remote when it's placed on the table. In order to reach it, they have to build up enough momentum in their rocking chair to lean forward and grab it. That's hard if you've got arthritis.

The solution: Connect a V8 engine to it!

Does it work? No. The V8 engine will cause the rocking chair to collapse and the old lady to disintegrate into many pieces.

Conclusion: Sturdier rocking chair and old lady needed.

Leg coming off

Alligator vs Crocodile

On their big American road trip, the boys did their best to keep out of a river infested by alligators. Or maybe crocodiles. They're tricky to tell apart, but with this guide you'll know exactly which toothy reptile is chasing you...

Snouts: The crocodile has a long, narrow nose, while the alligator's snout is flatter and wider.

Teeth: The teeth on a crocodile's upper and lower jaws lock together neatly when its mouth is closed, while an alligator's lower teeth are hidden from view. A crocodile has a huge 'fourth tooth' on its lower jaw, which is not visible on an alligator.

Alligators

Crocodile

Size: Crocodiles are larger than alligators. They will often reach six metres in length, while alligators rarely grow longer than four metres.

Colour: Crocodiles are usually brownish and lighter in colour than alligators, which appear more black. However, this isn't much help unless you have one of each side-by-side!

Angriness: Crocodiles are usually regarded as more aggressive than alligators. However, if you spot either in your neighbourhood, it's best to run quickly in the opposite direction!

Hammond? **Alligators**, mate.

We may have made them angry, I've just driven into their **living room**.

Who is Jackie Stewart?

Back in 2006, a mysterious man in a checked cap turned Captain Slow into a proper racing driver in a TVR Tuscan. But who was he?

Jackie Stewart is one of the most famous Formula One drivers of all time. He won three world championships in the 1960s and 70s, when crashes would claim drivers' lives on a weekly basis.

In total, Jackie Stewart won twenty-seven F1 races and finished on the podium forty-five times. He raced in exactly 100 Grands Prix.

His most famous F1 win came in 1968 at the terrifying Nürburgring. In pouring rain, driving with a broken wrist, he won the race by more than four minutes.

In the Belgian Grand Prix in 1966, Stewart crashed at 165mph and hit a telegraph pole.

He was trapped in his car for twenty-five minutes before help arrived. After this experience, he became a passionate campaigner for better safety in F1.

Before Stewart's campaigning, F1 drivers were not required to wear seatbelts or a full-face helmet.

Thanks to improvements in track and car safety, there has not been a fatal accident in F1 since 1994. Much of this is thanks to Jackie Stewart.

All that, and he managed to knock twenty seconds off James May's lap time!

More power, more power... **Full** power! **Full power!** Don't put the power on until you know you'll **never** have to take it off.

British Racing Drivers

Some of these chaps you may have heard of. Some of them your Dad – or your granddad – may go on about. But are the new guys better than the old ones? Who knows – that's what arguing is for.

Martin Brundle b. 1959. Raced with Ayrton Senna in the British Formula Three Championship in 1983, then moved up to F1. Won the World Sportscar Championship in 1988 and the Le Mans 24 Hours race in 1989. Now a respected commentator.

Richard Burns 1971–2005. World Rally Champion in 2001, runner-up in 1999 and 2000. Lived near, and knew, Jeremy Clarkson. Sadly died of a brain tumour.

Jenson Button MBE b. 1980. F1 driver since 2000, won the World Drivers' Championship in 2009.

Jim Clark 1936-68, Scotland. When he died, he had twenty-five Grand Prix wins and achieved thirty-three Grand Prix pole positions – more than any other driver at the time. Had the natural skill to drive any car he got in to. He raced in hill climbs, British Touring Car Championships, the RAC Rally, the Le Mans 24 Hour race, NASCAR and the Indianapolis 500.

David Coulthard b. 1971, Scotland. Thirteen Grand Prix wins as an F1 driver; won the highest points total for a British driver. Now races in the German DTM series.

Lewis Hamilton MBE b. 1985. Started in Formula Renault and Formula Three. Won GP2 in his first year (2006). Moved up to F1 in 2007. In 2008 he became the youngest ever F1 World Champion.

Tim Harvey b. 1961. BTCC driver 1987–2002, champion in 1992. Many wins in other competitions; still racing, and commentating.

Mike Hawthorn 1929–1959. F1 driver 1952–1958, World Drivers Champion 1958. Won the 24 Hours of Le Mans in 1955. The Hawthorn Memorial Trophy is given each year to the most successful British or Commonwealth F1 driver.

Damon Hill OBE b. 1960. Started racing motorbikes, then Formula Ford and Formula 3000. Raced F1 1992 –1999, winning the World Drivers' Championship in 1996. Graham Hill's son.

Graham Hill 1929–1975. F1 driver 1958–1975, World Drivers' Champion in 1962 and 1968. The only driver ever to win the Indianapolis 500, the Monaco Grand Prix and the Le Mans 24 Hours and owner of the coolest moustache in motor sport.

Paddy Hopkirk b. 1933, N. Ireland. Won the 1964 Monte Carlo Rally in a Mini Cooper S. No British crew has won there since.

James Hunt 1947–1993. Started in touring car racing, then Formula Three, and F1 from 1973 to 1979. World Drivers' Champion in 1976. Very popular and entertaining both as a racing driver and as a commentator. Won F1 in 1976.

Eddie Irvine b. 1965, N. Ireland. Raced Formula Ford, Formula 3 and Formula 3000 before F1 from 1993–2002. Charismatic and wealthy – friends with Bono, went out with Pamela Anderson.

Nigel Mansell OBE b. 1953. The most successful British F1 driver so far (thirty-one wins between 1980 and 1995) and World Drivers' Champion in 1992. He also won the 1993 CART IndyCar World Series. He continues to be heavily involved in racing, and advertising insurance.

Stirling Moss OBE b. 1929. Raced from 1948 to 1962, winning 212 of the 529 races he entered, including 16 F1 Grands Prix. Drove dozens of different makes of car. His younger sister Pat won the European Ladies Rally Champion five times.

Matt Neal b. 1966. BTCC driver since 1991, won in 2005 and 2006. In 2005 he completed all thirty BTCC races, which no one else has ever managed. Raced a motorhome against Richard Hammond. Remarkably, taller than Jeremy Clarkson.

Richard Noble OBE b. 1946, Scotland. Held the land speed record from 1983 to 1997 (at 633mph). Project director of ThrustSSC, which holds the current speed record – 763mph.

Tiff Needell b. 1951. Has raced Formula Ford, Formula 3, F1 (briefly), British Rallycross, 24 Hours of Le Mans, BTCC and many others. Presenter on *Fifth Gear*; used to present an old motoring show called, er, *Top Gear*.

Andy Priaulx b. 1973, Guernsey. ETCC champion, three times WTCC champion. Won British Hillclimb Championship in 1995.

Colin McRae MBE 1968-2007, Scotland. British Rally Champion 1991 and 1992. In 1995 he was the youngest man – and first ever Brit – to win the WRC Drivers competition. Also completed the 24 Hours of Le Mans and the Dakar Rally. Sadly died in helicopter accident in 2007.

Jason Plato b. 1967. BTCC champion in 2001 & 2010. *Fifth Gear* presenter.

Anthony Read b. 1957, Scotland. BTCC driver since 1997. Won Hammond's bus race; second in the airport vehicles race.

Jackie Stewart OBE b. 1939, Scotland. F1 driver from 165 to 1973, winning three World Drivers' Championships. After leaving F1 he campaigned for better safety at Grand Prix circuits, and became a commentator and team owner. Taught James May to drive faster.

John Surtees OBE b. 1934. Raced motorbikes and cars – the only man to win World Championships on two and four wheels. Dominated Grand Prix motorcycle racing from 1956 to 1960, when he switched to F1 until 1972. World Drivers' Champion in 1964.

Colin Turkington b. 1982, N. Ireland. BTCC driver since 2002. Winner in 2009. Now competing in the WTCC.

Car Washes – What Not to Do

DO

- **Close all the windows.**

- **Retract the aerial (if you can).**

- **Turn off the engine.**

- **Read all the other instructions and do what they say.**

The thing is, we managed to set **fire** to something that's basically made of **water!**

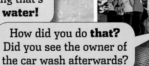

How did you do **that?** Did you see the owner of the car wash afterwards?

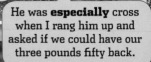

He was...

Cross. Very cross.

He was **especially** cross when I rang him up and asked if we could have our three pounds fifty back.

DON'T

- **Go in with a car you made yourself.**

- **Get out and run away halfway through.**

Uh... it's **on fire.**

What?! It **can't** be on fire! It's on fire.

It's on fire. Just **run.** Just **run.**

- **Get bits of your home-made car stuck in the carwash and set it on fire**

- **Let the Stig anywhere near one.**

Car Gadgets to Make your Life 'Better'

Over the years the chaps have come across various bits and bobs that car companies think you would like, or that are meant to improve your motoring experience. And you know what? Without exception, they're all... **useless**. For example:

Have you **ever** thought, 'Oh no, my shoehorn is too heavy!' How about a shoehorn made of **carbon fibre**? No? Thought not.

- A sink plunger made from the gear stick of a Ferrari. Only £17 – a bargain!
- A NASCAR sofa embroidered with the signature of Geoff Gordon (whoever he is) for £1,300
- Ineffective little clip-on fans that just push the hot air at you faster, and then fall off
- Air fresheners, to add the delicious authentic smell of industrial chemicals to the unpleasant stink you're trying to hide
- Bugatti aftershave costing £1,500. Richard: 'An original fragrance shrouded in mystery with underlying notes of patchouli, cedarwood and vetivert.' It comes with a metal sculpture in a carbon fibre case

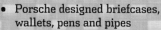

- A red plastic Ferrari sledge for £50
- A wobbly-headed model of the former president of Nissan USA. (The head comes off a bit easily.)
- Nissan bar stool and guitar
- Lamborghini baubles for your Christmas tree

- Porsche designed briefcases, wallets, pens and pipes
- An eco calculator from Renault, which you shake to make it work
- A plastic surround for an ashtray shaped like a disc brake and caliper

- Belt-mounted smoker's pouch with MG branding
- MG socks, underpants, overnight bag, slippers, hat, jumper, apron, scarf... Richard tried them all on at once

- A Saab ice scraper – £38.50
- Land Rover distress whistle (£1) that sounds like a mouse squeaking
- Mercedes-Benz shirt with the web address sewn into the collar
- A fork with a 10mm ring spanner at the other end, so you can go seamlessly from mending a motorcycle to eating a pie
- A gizmo you fix to your exhaust and it kind of makes the sound of a turbo. Won't fool anyone fixed to a Fiat Panda, though
- A handbag made from the seatcloth of a classic Camaro (so a sweaty American has sat on it for years)
- RAC 'eau de voiture' – aftershave for your car, for that authentic aroma of minicab

- Porsche-designed trainers – a bargain at £310

- Bacon-scented air freshener. Mmmm!
- A vest with 'TRUCKER' written on it, from Mercedes-Benz.
- A dimmer switch shaped like a Bugatti Veyron
- Nail clippers shaped like a car
- A clock mounted on a little steering wheel
- Drinks coasters shaped like steering wheels
- A bottle stopper or a toothpick holder shaped like a gearstick

What is a Muscle Car?

Top Gear loves muscle cars, but what exactly are they? Here's a quick history of America's favourite tyre-smokin', gas-burnin' automobiles...

Old Dodge Challenger

Muscle cars were born in the 1950s in the USA. The aim was simple: to stick a big engine in a smallish, cheap car to create a machine of speed for a reasonable price.

The engine of choice for muscle cars has always been a big V8 – an engine still found today in many performance and supercars... and Jeremy's blender!

Muscle cars are always rear-wheel drive and usually overpowered. This means that they will smoke their tyres if the driver gets busy with the accelerator!

Chevrolet Camaro

New Dodge Challenger

The golden era for the muscle car was the 1960s, when big American manufacturers battled for victory on the road and the drag strip. It was in this era that the most legendary muscle cars were born, including the Chevrolet Camaro, Dodge Challenger and Ford Mustang. These cars are still produced today, though they are far safer and better equipped than their 1960s predecessors!

Pontiac Firebird

Traditional muscle cars tended to have hugely powerful engines but very poor brakes and handling. In other words, they'd go down a straight road like a bolt of lightning, but encounter a corner and you'd be in trouble!

Other countries, including Britain and Australia, have produced muscle cars. Some of the most famous modern examples are produced by Australian brand Holden, which reach the UK as the Vauxhall Monaro and VXR8.

Vauxhall Monaro

Things Measured in Jeremys

Jeremy is 1.98m (6ft 6in) tall. If this distance is one jeremy, then...

The tallest man in the world (Robert Wadlow)
1.37 jeremys tall

Jeremy Clarkson
1 jeremy tall

Empire State Building
224 jeremys tall

Eiffel Tower
152 jeremys tall

Statue of Liberty
47 jeremys tall

London Eye
68 jeremys tall

One lap of the Nürburgring
11.52 kilojeremys

Laerdal Tunnel in Norway
12.37 kilojeremys long

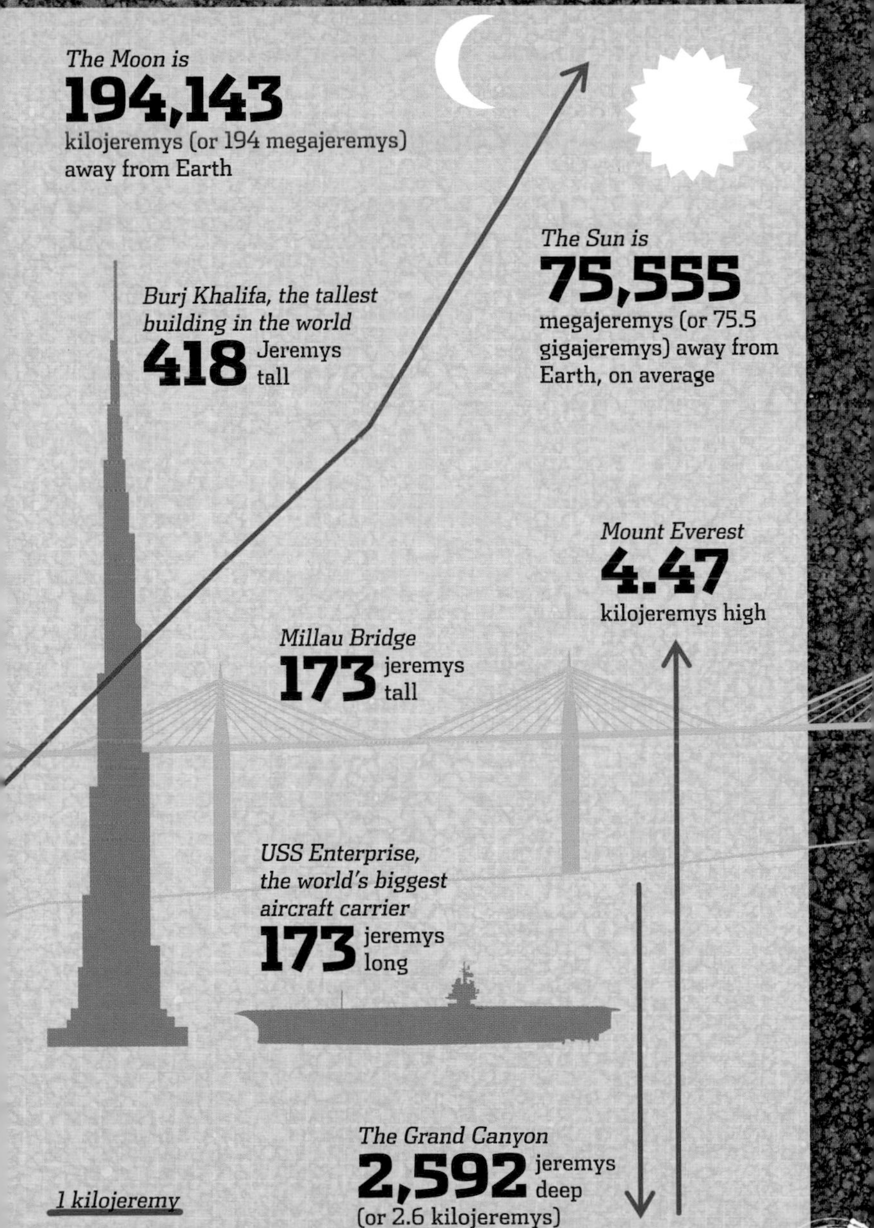

The Moon is
194,143
kilojeremys (or 194 megajeremys)
away from Earth

The Sun is
75,555
megajeremys (or 75.5
gigajeremys) away from
Earth, on average

Burj Khalifa, the tallest
building in the world
418 Jeremys
tall

Mount Everest
4.47
kilojeremys high

Millau Bridge
173 jeremys
tall

USS Enterprise,
the world's biggest
aircraft carrier
173 jeremys
long

The Grand Canyon
2,592 jeremys
deep
(or 2.6 kilojeremys)

1 kilojeremy

Odd Vehicle Races and What We Can Learn from Them

Motorhomes

Traditionally, amateur drivers going off for a weekend of racing tow their car behind a motorhome, which they sleep in. Richard thought, why not save time and weight by leaving the car and trailer behind, and racing the motorhome – after sleeping in it?

'I think this plan has the stench of genius about it.'

Competitors are a variety of sizes and shapes, which makes the race unpredictable and therefore entertaining. And, according to the Official Rules of Motorhome Racing 2007*, the vehicles have to be prepared for racing before the sun goes down on the day before the race. Do you strip out the fittings to save weight, and have a rubbish night's sleep? Or leave the bed and cooker in, sleep well, but have to drive a tank?

The motorhome drivers
- Richard: Ford Midas
- Matt Neal: Mitsubishi L300
- Anthony Reid: Toyota Lite Ace
- Tom Chilton: big Chevrolet A-class
- Mat Jackson: LHD Fiat Ducato NV70 Globetrotter
- James May: Ford Transit

Richard went for the Strip-It-All-Out-Have-A-Bad-Night option. As did everyone else – apart from James, who was able to cook a lovely pie with potatoes, peas and gravy.

The Rules also stated that *no contact* was allowed during the race, in order for competitors to be able to drive home afterwards. Somehow everyone forgot this rule. Only four vehicles made it over the line, and Richard's Ford looked a bit sad and, er, broken.

CONCLUSION: Amateur racing works fine already thanks, Richard.

Buses

Choosing a new bus for your city is normally a tricky business. You need to have lots of meetings about costs, emissions, safety, passenger preference and all that kind of thing. Or you could just have a race, and pick the winner.

---

* Written on the back of an envelope by Richard

The bus drivers
- Tom Chilton: Leyland Olympia double-decker
- Anthony Reid: Dennis Dart single-decker
- Gordon Sheddon: Mercedes O305G bendybus
- Matt Neil: MetroRider compact city hopper
- Richard: another bendybus, as they seemed the most likely to cause trouble

As Richard put it: 'The ultimate crucible of excellence – motorsport. For anything on four wheels, this is the white heat of the anvil of the spearhead of evolution.' (Eh?)

In the interest of important investigative research, the drivers agreed on a no-contact rule. This lasted for almost half a lap. The single-seater may not have had as many seats as some of the others, but it proved fast enough to skid round corners, tip the double-decker over, rip Richard's tyres off and win the race.

CONCLUSION: All cities should just use single-decker buses, because they're fastest.

Airport vehicles

Air travel is very boring, because of all the slooooow vehicles doing things like loading the luggage and shunting the planes about. Time for TG to step in and decide which should be allowed to survive, and which should be retired.

No contact was essential for a fair test. So they immediately started doofing each other off the track. The heavy plane tug was soon left in the dust. The fuel tanker mashed into the luggage truck.

Once he'd shed some weight, Richard crippled the bendy bus, while the steps and the catering truck toppled over on a sharp bend – leaving the fire engine to win.

The airport drivers
- Tom Chilton: Mobile aircraft steps
- Gordon Shedden: Bendybus
- Mat Jackson: Plane tug
- Stuart Oliver: Fuel tanker
- Anthony Reid: Catering truck
- Matt Neal: Luggage truck and four luggage trolleys
- Richard: Fire engine

CONCLUSION: All airport vehicles should be fire engines, but only if they dump the eight tonnes of water first.

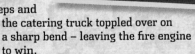

Car Terms Explained

Attention car geeks! Here's an incomplete and poorly explained list of car terms that Jeremy likes to use in his sensible, considered car reviews.

4X4 'Four by four' means a vehicle has four powered wheels. It may be possible to turn the power off to some wheels.

ABS Anti-lock Braking System. When braking on a slippery surface, the wheels can lock – stop turning – and skid. ABS sensors in each wheel spot when it's about to lock and ease off that wheel's brake. When the wheel turns again, the brake goes back on. This happens many times a second, and the effect is felt by the driver as a juddering, noisy brake pedal.

BTCC British Touring Car Championship, a useful source of drivers for Richard's alternative races (see page 152)

Carb/carburettor A gizmo you get in older cars to mix fuel with air before it gets sucked into the engine's cylinders. Since the early 1990s, most cars have direct fuel injection instead.

Carbon fibre Expensive fibreglass. It's used in cars and bikes because it's strong for its weight (thanks to the strands of carbon in it). And because it's a bit flash.

Cat/catalytic converter A box which turns some of the nasty stuff in the exhaust into less-nasty stuff. Because cats are full of very expensive metals, thieves have got rather good at nicking them off SUVs (which are big enough to crawl under).

CC Cubic centimetres, a measure of the total volume of an engine's cylinders. There are 1000cc in a litre.

Chassis A car's skeleton, that holds all the moving bits (organs) in place and supports the surface panels (skin).

Crankshaft This is a wiggly-shaped rod that the pistons are linked to, that turns their up-and-down movement to a round-and-round movement, which is what you want to make the wheels turn. It's a bit like a row of bike pedals, with pistons instead of your legs.

Diff/differential The engine spins a propshaft, which leads in to a clever collection of gearwheels called the diff. This splits the engine's power between two wheels, so when one needs to turn faster (to get round the longer outside edge of a bend) it can. But if one wheel is on a slippery surface like mud or ice, it goes wrong. The diff provides enough power to spin the slipping wheel, but delivers the *same* power to the other wheel – which won't be enough to move it. A **limited-slip diff** is clever enough to work out that the non-slipping wheel needs *more* power than the slipping

one, and gives it. An **active diff** (found in cars like the Ferrari F430 and the Mitsubishi Evo) uses a computer and sensors to adjust power to each wheel, giving each of them the most it can cope with without slipping. Four-wheel-drive vehicles have a diff on both axles, and usually another centre diff as well. Greedy.

Distributor This distributes electricity to the sparkplugs, one after another in a particular order, at exactly the right moment. There are leads running from the distributor cap to the plugs, which can come loose.

Dual overhead cams This is getting very geeky! The camshaft is a rod that turns in time with the crankshaft, with bumps on it which open the valves at the top of each cylinder (to let air in and exhaust out). Flashy engines have four valves on each cylinder, which needs two cams for some reason that only James knows.

Flappy paddle gears Rather than moving a rod which physically shifts the gears, you flick a lever and a computer does it for you, only much quicker. It took about four years for Jeremy to stop complaining about these.

G gravity, specifically Earth's gravity. Or, to put it another way, 'how heavy something feels'. If you experience 2G as a car corners or on a rollercoaster, you feel twice as heavy.

Gasket The join or seal between a cylinder, where a piston slides up and down, and the cylinder head, where the sparkplug and valves do their business. When a rubbish old car 'blows a gasket' it loses power and makes a lot of noise.

GT Grand Tourer – a big, comfortable car you can drive across Europe without getting a numb bum.

HP Horsepower. A unit measurement of an engine's power, like metre is a unit measurement of distance. It was developed to work out how good engines were at doing work previously done by horses. 1hp is about 740W – the same as a small microwave.

Intercooler – the air coming out of a turbocharger has been squashed, so it contains more oxygen, but it has also got hot. An intercooler cools the air down before it goes into the engine, making it give an even bigger bang.

Manifold Some of the tubes that are fixed to an engine. There's some to put air in it, and some to get exhaust out.

Monocoque A car without a chassis, which saves weight. Think of it as a very strong egg, or a crab. All the bits holding it together are on the outside, rather than the inside.

Oversteer You turn the wheel to go round a corner, and the car turns more than you expected (usually because the rear-wheel drive has made the back skid outwards).

Revs Revolutions per minute. The second hand on a watch moves at 1 rev. Car engines can do 10,000 revs. The bit that's revolving (pushed round by the pistons) is the crankshaft, which turns (via the gearbox, propshaft and diff) the wheels. 'Revving' an engine means pressing the accelerator to make it turn faster (and get louder).

RS Rally Sport. Or RennSport, if you're German, which translates as 'racing sport'. If a car's got RS in its name, it's probably pretty quick.

RWD Rear-Wheel Drive. Guess what FWD means.

Splitter Like a spoiler, but underneath on the front instead of on the top at the back.

Spoiler A little wing. As you drive along, air pushes on the spoiler, which pushes the car down onto the road, making it grip better.

Supercharger This does the same thing as a turbocharger, but is powered by the engine rather than the exhaust.

Suspension When one of your car's wheels goes over a bump, you want just that wheel to move up over it, not the whole car. Jeremy prefers independent suspension, where each wheel can move separately, to fixed or linked suspension. Some cars have active suspension, where computers control things so the car corners, brakes and accelerates better.

SUV Sports Utility Vehicle, a bloated overpriced mumvan that's probably useless off-road.

SV Sport Veloce, what Lamborghini put on their *really* fast cars.

Throttle Also known as the gas, wick, beans or accelerator. Pressing a pedal with your right foot makes the engine suck in more air and fuel, so it produces more power and makes the car speed up. Simple really.

Torque The turning force an engine applies. Torque multiplied by engine revs equals horsepower. So a big truck and a hot hatch may measure the same hp, but the truck produces more torque (to move a heavy load) while the car produces more revs (to go faster). Cars usually produce the most torque – accelerate hardest – over a small range of engine revs.

Torque Steer A powerful engine in a front-wheel-drive car can make the car pull over to one side when it speeds up.

Traction Control A computer that stops you skidding, by sensing when the wheels are losing grip, and then slowing them down a bit. The Stig likes to turn it off.

Turbo/turbocharger A pump (powered by the exhaust) that squashes the air going into the engine, so it contains more oxygen. This makes the engine produce more power. Turbos can spin at 150,000 revs!

Turbo lag A turbo can't kick in and deliver a power boost until it speeds up a bit, so there can be a wait after mashing the accelerator pedal before the car leaps forward. Some cars get round this by having two turbos – a little one that gets going quickly, and a bigger one to take over when the revs have gone up enough.

Understeer You turn the wheel to go round a corner, and the car doesn't turn as much as you expected (usually because the front-wheel-drive is still trying to pull the car forwards, rather than turning).

And on that bombshell... goodnight!